NEW ZEALAND

FOOD
WINE &ART

A NEW JOURNEY

NEW ZEALAND

FOOD
& WINE ART

A NEW JOURNEY

Photography: Ian Baker
Text: Vic Williams

with Anne-Marie Davis and Carol Hunter

CHANEL

ACKNOWLEDGEMENTS

New Zealand Food Wine & Art – A New Journey was conceived by the publisher, photographer and many of the team who worked on the previous edition.

Our major thanks to the chefs, restaurants and wineries who have supplied recipes and were so accommodating with their time. A Restaurant Directory can be found on page 192.

A special thank you to the artists and galleries who have generously given permission to reproduce the artworks, especially Kura, Taupo. A list of Artists, Agents and Outlets can be found on page 190.

My grateful thanks to the team who helped put this book together: Ian Baker, who photographed the previous book, and has again provided stimulating pictures of food, scenery and artworks; Vic Williams who helped with wine suggestions for many of the dishes, adapted the recipes for home use and wrote the text; Lesley Coomer for her creative design and layout and the long hours spent reshaping the book with Barbara and Ian; the production and editorial team headed by Barbara Nielsen of Stylus Publishing Services, who have produced a splendid book; Anne-Marie Davis, and Carol Hunter, who assisted Ian to select the range of artists for this book and researched and wrote the art captions; and my assistant Robin Falconer who was invaluable in liaising with the restaurants.

To Joan Mackenzie and her colleagues at Whitcoulls – thank you for having faith in the book.

Cliff Josephs

Photographs on preliminary pages: endpapers, countryside near Hanmer Springs;
half title page, *Driving Creek* by Louis Kittleson; title page, Lake Wakatipu, Queenstown.

Chanel Publishers Ltd
P.O. Box 403, Whangaparaoa

First published by Chanel Publishers Ltd, 2002
Copyright © Photography: Ian Baker
Text: Chanel Publishers Ltd
Recipes: Remain with the contributing restaurants

Publisher: Cliff Josephs
Photographer: Ian Baker
Text writer: Vic Williams
Recipe editor and researcher: Vic Williams
Art advisors and writers: Anne-Marie Davis and Carol Hunter
Production manager: Barbara Nielsen
Design and layout: Lesley Coomer
Editorial team: Alison Dench, Nicola Farquhar, Fiona McRae
Map artwork: Pauline Whimp
Indexer: Diane Lowther
Researcher: Robin Falconer
Printed by: Midas Printing (Asia) Ltd

ISBN: 0-958208-46-8

CONTENTS

INTRODUCTION

New Zealand Food Wine & Art was recognised by Booksellers New Zealand as the bestselling New Zealand book for 2001. In publishing a new book on food, wine and art we wondered briefly whether it could be as good as the first. We are, however, fortunate to be living in a country where the food, wine and art industries are developing rapidly. This made our new effort very much easier, which is why we have titled it *New Zealand Food Wine & Art – A New Journey*.

Our new edition covers new restaurants and old favourites, all with new recipes and wine recommendations and all photographed by Ian Baker.

Ian combined the food with local scenic delights, and the artworks pictured by him have been selected to provide a sampling of the styles and creativity in each region. Ian says: 'It was wonderful to have the opportunity to travel again throughout the country sampling the evolving styles of cooking and presentation. I also welcomed the chance to include wines that we were unable to feature in the last edition and to explore the varied work of artists, some of whom are not yet well known outside the localities in which they work.'

In *New Zealand Food Wine & Art – A New Journey* we are fortunate to have Vic Williams, food and wine writer, join us to work with the chefs in editing the recipes and to write the descriptive text and help with wine suggestions. Vic says he found the project immensely exciting. 'New Zealand has some of the most creative chefs in the world, but their innovation is tempered by a real respect for the ingredients. The dishes in this book were chosen because they speak clearly of their respective regions. Some are new creations, others are classics – but they and the wines chosen to accompany them all vividly reflect the land we love. New Zealand wine is now known internationally. Many of the styles that have helped put our tiny country on the map are featured in this book.'

Once again I would like to thank the chefs, wineries and artists who have allowed us to showcase their talents and bring the reader a new and unique look at our country's taste and artistry.

Cliff Josephs

PUBLISHER

Cape Reinga

Bay of Islands

South Pacific Ocean

Waitangi • Paihia
Kawakawa

Northland

WHANGAREI

Dargaville

Waiheke Island

Warkworth

Coromandel

*Coromandel &
Bay of Plenty*

AUCKLAND

Whitianga

Auckland

Mt Maunganui

TAURANGA
Te Puke

HAMILTON

ROTORUA

*Waikato,
Central Plateau
& Taranaki*

TAUPO

GISBORNE

Wairoa

NEW PLYMOUTH

NAPIER

HASTINGS

*Hawke's Bay,
Manawatu
& Wanganui*

Tasman Sea

WANGANUI

PALMERSTON NORTH
Dannevirke

Foxton

Waikanae

Masterton

Lower Hutt
Martinborough

*Wairarapa
& Wellington*

*Nelson
& Marlborough*

WELLINGTON

PICTON
Cook Strait

NELSON
Richmond
BLENHEIM
Renwick

Westport

West Coast

Kaikoura

GREYMOUTH

Hokitika

Amberley

Franz Josef

CHRISTCHURCH

*Kaikoura &
Canterbury*

TIMARU

QUEENSTOWN
Clyde

South Pacific Ocean

N

*Queenstown
& Central Otago*

DUNEDIN

INVERCARGILL
*Otago
& Southland*

Riverton

Half Moon Bay

STEWART ISLAND

Sun, Sand and Salt Winds

Northland

*T*hey call it 'the winterless north', and certainly this part of New Zealand has more than its share of warm, bright days.

But there is a flip side. Much of the region comes within the influence of its two bordering oceans, and they have played a major part in shaping the landscape over the centuries. Storms roar unimpeded across the narrower pieces of land, leaving a legacy of leaning trees and nutrient-stripped soil.

Proximity to the ocean means that seafood plays an important part on many restaurant menus, but chefs also have access to excellent locally bred beef, lamb, pork, ostrich and poultry.

And not all the soil has been devitalised by the elements. Tropical fruits and vegetables perform better than they do anywhere else in the country, and Northland forests are dense and spectacular.

Wineries in the far north can be counted on the fingers of one hand but, closer to Auckland, Matakana and its surrounding districts are producing some of the most exciting wines in the land.

The area played an important part in New Zealand's formation. The Treaty of Waitangi, the sometimes controversial agreement between Maori and representatives of the British Crown, was signed in the region in 1840 and still plays an important role in society today.

Art has been part of the local scene for a very long time. Excellent examples of Maori carving abound, together with modern interpretations of ancient ideas from Kerry Kapuna Thompson and others. Local artists of European descent often call on the original inhabitants for inspiration. The land is almost invariably a focus, directly in the case of the clay shapes of Robyn Stewart and the constructions of English expatriate, Peter Oxborough, and by association in the colourfully evocative oils of Carrie Henderson.

Lush forests, spectacular beaches and a past that has strong links with the present day – Northland is a vital part of New Zealand, and a must on any traveller's itinerary.

A view from Cape Reinga looking south.

Tandoori Veal Cutlets

with garlic roti and lima bean aïoli

4 teaspoons cumin seeds
2cm cinnamon quill
1 teaspoon ground cloves
2 teaspoons chilli powder
2 teaspoons ground ginger
2 teaspoons turmeric powder
2 teaspoons garlic powder
2 teaspoons mace
2 teaspoons kosher salt
¹/₂ teaspoon powdered red food colouring
(available at Asian food stores)
12 veal cutlets

Dry-fry the first three ingredients in a cast-iron frypan until they begin to smoke. Cool, combine with the powdered spices and grind in a coffee grinder or mortar and pestle along with the salt and food colouring. Add sufficient cold water to make a light paste and smear over and around the cutlets in a bowl. Marinate for 2 hours, then drain and pat dry.

Salad
1 eggplant (aubergine)
olive oil for grilling
24 asparagus spears
18 snow peas
9 shiitake mushrooms
24 semi-dried tomatoes (available at good delicatessens)
18 sprigs fresh coriander

Cut the eggplant lengthwise into six slices, then halve each slice lengthwise to give you twelve pieces. Brush with olive oil and grill until soft and lightly browned. Peel the asparagus spears from a point 1cm below the start of the 'flower' and snap off the stem where it becomes hard. Trim to make all the spears approximately the same length. Blanch in salted water until tender but still brightly coloured. Trim the snow peas if necessary and blanch for a few seconds. Cut the shiitake mushrooms into thin strips and pan-fry in a little olive oil.

To complete and serve
6 garlic roti breads (available at Asian food stores and some supermarkets)
Lima Bean Aïoli (see page 188)

Heat the roti breads in a warm oven. Place one in the centre of each plate and top with most of the salad ingredients, putting aside one piece of eggplant and a few other components. Place two veal cutlets on each plate and scatter the reserved eggplant slices and remaining salad on top. Drizzle the Lima Bean Aïoli around the edge.

Serves 6
Recommended wine:
Stonyridge Larose

Recipe from Henrick Wessenaar
KAURI CLIFFS LODGE
MATAURI BAY

Above: The view of the coast from the golf course at Kauri Cliffs.

Below: Mahe is a carved, hand-burnished and fired mahe or anchor stone by Robyn Stewart. Robyn's clay carvings are sculptural in form. Some pieces are hand-built vessel forms while others rely completely on the 'gift of fire' for decoration. Robyn's work is influenced by the Northland environment where she lives surrounded by native bush and close to the sea.

Barbecued Chicken Breast

with fennel and orange polenta, celery and green pea sauce

Chicken
6 skinless chicken breasts

Trim the chicken breasts of all fat and skin particles. If the fillets have been left attached, pull out and discard the wedge-ended white tendon that runs the length of each. Pat dry with paper towels and refrigerate until needed.

Fennel and Orange Polenta
1 tablespoon fennel seeds
1 small onion
1 tablespoon orange zest
1 teaspoon chopped fresh or ¹/₂ teaspoon dried sage
1 teaspoon chopped fresh or ¹/₂ teaspoon dried thyme
500ml chicken stock or water
500ml milk
2 tablespoons extra virgin olive oil
330g fine-grained polenta
1 tablespoon butter
¹/₂ cup grated parmesan cheese (freshly grated is best)
salt and pepper to taste
Cajun Spice Mix (see page 188)
Celery and Green Pea Sauce (see page 188)

Dry-fry the fennel seeds. Finely dice the onion. Place the first seven ingredients in a heavy saucepan and bring gradually to a simmer (slow heating gives the flavours more time to infuse). Meanwhile, brush a shallow baking dish with one tablespoon of the oil and line with plastic food wrap. When the liquid is simmering sprinkle in the polenta and heat, stirring with a wooden spoon to knock out any lumps (be careful – the mixture will spit). Cook over low heat for approximately 10 minutes, stirring regularly. Add the butter, remaining olive oil and cheese. Stir to mix, then add salt and pepper to taste. The texture should

be like thick porridge. Spoon into the prepared baking dish and use the spoon to spread it evenly. Wet your hands with cold water and press the mixture until it is completely smooth and about 1cm thick. Remember that any cracks or fractures will break when it is cut, so be sure to eliminate them. Cover with plastic food wrap and refrigerate until firm.

To complete and serve
Spread some of the Cajun Spice Mix on a plate and press the chicken breasts into it. Heat a barbecue and cook the breasts over medium heat, being careful not to blacken the coating too much. Using a pan lid or roasting tray to cover the breasts will speed up the cooking time and allow them to part-steam. Turn regularly. They should be firm and cooked after about 20 minutes, but make sure by slicing one from thin end to thick. If it is still slightly pink, slice the other pieces and place them cut-side down for a further 2–3 minutes.

Meanwhile, turn the polenta out onto a chopping block and cut into even triangles. Brush lightly with oil and season with salt and pepper. Cook on the barbecue, turning 45 degrees halfway through to achieve a criss-cross pattern. Do the same on both sides.

To serve, fan two or three polenta triangles on each plate, arrange the sliced chicken breasts on top and drizzle the Celery and Green Pea Sauce over and around both.

The dish, as photographed, is garnished with a salad of baby greens, celery leaves, fennel, red onion and parmesan, all tossed in extra virgin olive oil. Restaurateurs Mark and Lyn Oliver stress that this recipe is simply a guide. 'Have fun – let your taste buds guide you. Modify the basic polenta any way you like. Try using barbecued eggplant, capsicum, courgette, garlic and chopped fresh basil instead of our flavourings. If you like, it can be fried instead of barbecued to give it a crisp surface.'

They also suggest increasing or

decreasing the chilli component of the spice mix, or adding brown sugar to give a caramel flavour (and a blacker colour to the finished dish). The spice mix keeps well in a sealed jar, and can be used on anything grilled – fish, lamb, beef or chicken wings.

Serves 6
Recommended wine:
Okahu Estate Proprietor's Reserve Chardonnay
Recipe from Mark and Lyn Oliver

MARX RESTAURANT
KERIKERI

Above left: Ebbing Estuary Top Sail *(ceramic and driftwood).*
Above right: Marker *(ceramic and driftwood).*
Originally from England, but now living and working on the Te Kapa estuary, Peter Oxborough creates sculptural work that reflects his passion for the environment – the sea, the beach and sailing boats. Wood-fired ceramic pieces combined with found items collected while out sailing are a recurring feature of his work.

Above: Scarlet pohutukawa blossoms frame the wharf at Russell. The pohutukawa is known as the New Zealand Christmas tree because it flowers throughout the summer months.

Below: In 2001 Whangarei-based Carolyn (Carrie) Henderson was selected to exhibit a collection of her works at The Mall Galleries in London. These figurative oil paintings on linen, The Pipi Pickers (left) and Northern Farm (right), depict scenes typical of the Northland region where she lives.

Steamed Mangonui Bluff Crayfish
with seared king prawns

1 whole live crayfish (see page 188 for preparation method)
2 king prawns
selection of summer fruits (rock melon, pawpaw, mango etc deseeded and diced)
1 small red chilli, deseeded and finely chopped
1 tablespoon chopped coriander
2 slices prosciutto (available at good delicatessens)
¹/₂ cup Béarnaise Sauce (see page 188)
2 teaspoons balsamic vinegar
5 tablespoons extra virgin olive oil
2 cups mesclun leaves

Remove and discard the shells from the prawns. Cut a fine groove down the back of each tail to expose the dark intestinal tract. Remove and discard.

Using a large Chinese bamboo steamer, steam the crayfish halves over boiling water until just cooked (about 7–8 minutes), adding the prawns for the last 2–3 minutes. Mix the fruit, chilli and coriander and pack into an egg ring or pastry cutter. Refrigerate until required.

Roughly chop the prosciutto and stir into the Béarnaise Sauce. Smear over the crayfish halves and brown under a hot grill. Shake the balsamic vinegar and olive oil together, season and toss with the mesclun leaves. Arrange the crayfish halves on a plate and place the prawns on top. Unmould the fruit alongside and garnish with the mesclun salad.

Serves 1
Recommended wine:
Mahurangi Estate Sauvignon Blanc

KAMAKURA
RUSSELL

BBQ Prawn Salad

1 tablespoon raisins
2 tablespoons balsamic vinegar
2 tablespoons pine nuts
5 whole green tiger prawns
Maldon sea salt
freshly ground black pepper
1 tablespoon Colonna mandarin-infused
olive oil (available from Sabato, Auckland)
$^1/_2$ cup rocket leaves
$^1/_2$ cup parmesan cheese shavings (parmigiano-
reggiano if possible), plus extra to garnish
1 tablespoon Lemon-infused Avocado Oil
(see page 188)
1 tablespoon Vincotto (available from Sabato,
Auckland)

Soak the raisins in the balsamic vinegar
for 48 hours. Dry-fry or grill the pine
nuts until golden. Remove and discard
the heads from the prawns, peel the
bodies and remove the black intestinal
vein that runs down the back. Season
with Maldon sea salt and black pepper,
drizzle with the mandarin-infused olive
oil and cook on a preheated barbecue
for 2 minutes each side. Place the rocket
leaves and half the parmesan shavings in
a bowl and toss with the avocado oil.

To complete and serve
Arrange the raisins and pine nuts on a
plate. Scatter half the rocket and
parmesan mixture on top, plus three
prawns. Complete with the remaining
ingredients. Finally, drizzle with Vincotto
and the remaining parmesan.

Serves 1
(Increase the prawns and salad according to
the number of servings, but be cautious with
the other ingredients)

Recommended wine:
Omata Estate Reserve Chardonnay

Recipe from Martin and Kay van Lubeck

OMATA ESTATE VINEYARD
BAY OF ISLANDS

Far left: Looking towards Paihia from the
Omata Estate Vineyard.

Corn and Coriander Fritters

with tomato salsa, sour cream and avocado

Fritters
420g tin creamed sweetcorn
2 eggs
2 tablespoons chopped fresh coriander leaves
1 1/2 cups plain flour
salt and pepper
6 egg whites
olive or other vegetable oil for frying

In a large bowl mix the corn, whole eggs and coriander. Add the flour in two lots, stirring vigorously after each addition. Season to taste. Next, whisk the egg whites until stiff and fold gently into the mixture.

Heat the oil to medium-high in a heavy frypan and add the mixture by the tablespoon. When golden-brown on one side (about 5 minutes), turn over and cook for a further 5 minutes. The fritters should be firm to touch.

Below: Born in Gisborne of Ngati Paoa descent, Kerry Kapuna Thompson carves contemporary works influenced by nature and based on traditional Maori design and legend. He uses bone, shell, jade and wood, and each piece is an original carving. This mask is made of mother-of-pearl shell.

Salsa
4 medium tomatoes
200g cucumber, peeled and deseeded
1 small red onion, peeled
zest and juice of 1 lemon
1 tablespoon chopped mint
salt and pepper to taste

Finely chop the tomatoes (discard the
seeds if they are very watery), cucumber
and onion, and mix with the other
ingredients. Refrigerate until needed
(the salsa can be made in advance, but
will become quite watery after a few hours).

To complete and serve
250ml sour cream
1 avocado, peeled and cut into 1cm cubes
fresh chives to garnish

Divide the Fritters between four plates
and top with the Salsa, sour cream and
avocado. Sprinkle the chives over the top.

Serves 4
Recommended wine:
Cottle Hill Sémillon/Chardonnay

Recipe from Hugh Blues
and Amanda Turner

WAIKOKOPU CAFE
PAIHIA

*Below: John Ecuyer's Pacific Offering
Vessel is wood-turned, incised and stained
purpleheart wood, embellished with silver,
brass and coconut shell beads.
John's vessel forms
have a multifaceted
appearance
and express
the often-
forgotten
aspects of our
modern lives. John
is a contemporary
wood turner who
produces distinctive
wood vessels reflecting
the art and culture
of the Pacific.*

KP's Flamed Seafood
bathed in a tomato, citrus and saffron jus with straw vegetables

4 cloves garlic
1 medium onion
2 stalks celery
2 courgettes (zucchini)
2–3 capsicums (peppers), variously coloured
1 large carrot
12 snow peas
1 medium tomato
6 good-sized live mussels
6 good-sized live surf clams (pipi or tuatua)
2 large crab claws
4 scallops
2 squid tubes
4 small fillets firm-fleshed fish like snapper,
gurnard or tarakihi
2 large prawns
4–6 pieces surimi (a good recipe-stretcher)
2 limes (preferably) or lemons
1 orange
2 tablespoons olive oil
2 tablespoons dry white wine
1 ¹/₂ cups tomato juice
pinch saffron
salt and freshly ground pepper
1–2 tablespoons extra virgin olive oil
coriander to garnish

Peel and finely chop the garlic and onion. Peel the celery and trim the ends off the courgettes. Remove the stems from the capsicums and discard the seeds and white ribs. Cut all the vegetables except the snow peas into matchstick-sized strips. Trim the snow peas if necessary. Dice the tomato. Pull the beards from the mussels and scrub both lots of shellfish, plus the crab claws. Remove and discard the hard 'boot' from the side of the scallops opposite the orange roe. Cut the squid tubes into rings, or open and flatten them, cross-hatch the inside and cut into 2cm squares. Cut the fish fillets into 2cm squares. Peel the prawns and remove the black intestinal vein that runs down the back, but leave the heads and tails attached. Slice the surimi. Zest the limes or lemons and the orange and squeeze the juice through a strainer into a bowl.

To complete and serve

Heat the olive oil in a large, heavy frypan or wok until it smokes. Throw in all the seafood, leaving the squid until last. If the pan flames, that's good (it imparts a smoky flavour), so if you're using gas, tip the pan to encourage it. Add the onion and garlic, plus a little more oil if necessary, then stir in the vegetables. Stir to soften slightly, then pour on the wine, the reserved zest and juice from the limes/lemons and orange, the tomato juice and saffron. After 3-4 minutes all the shellfish should be open, and the remaining seafood cooked. Add the diced tomato and season to taste. Place in heated bowls, drizzle with the extra virgin olive oil and garnish with the coriander leaves.

Note: If you are worried about the surf clams being sandy, steep them in cold water for an hour or so, changing the water frequently. As a last resort, they can be steamed open separately in a little water and white wine, rinsed of all traces of sand and added to the mixture just before serving. The catch is that rinsing robs them of some flavour. Farmed mussels are raised on poles suspended in clear water, so they are usually free of sand, but if you gather your own from sandy water you might like to give them the same treatment as the clams.

Serves 2 (generously!)
Recommended wine:
Cloudy Bay Sauvignon Blanc

Recipe from Owen Sinclair
KILLER PRAWN, WHANGAREI

Above: Willie Lassey is originally from Te-Awa Ngati Pokeko (Whakatane) and now lives in Whangarei. His Northland (oil on canvas) draws inspiration from music and works in a bold, figurative, contemporary style.

Above: Flax, a leaning pohutukawa and a curve of coast … the view from Whananaki is archetypal New Zealand.

Above top: Tane Mahuta, regal guardian of the Waipoua Forest, Northland. This giant kauri tree, an easy walk from the main road, attracts visitors from all over the world.

Above bottom: An accomplished weaver of traditional and contemporary kete, Jess Paraone creates exquisite work that reflects her respect for the traditions and spirituality that encompass the art of weaving. This kete is woven from dyed harakeke with rosebuds and emu feathers. Jess is of Nga Puhi descent.

Beef, Lamb and Oyster Pudding
with capsicum, olive and caper sauce

Pastry
250g plain flour
2 teaspoons baking powder
pinch salt
150g Shreddo (shredded suet)
cold water as required
butter for greasing ramekins

Sieve flour with baking powder and salt, add suet and cold water and mix until the mixture is very soft, but not too moist. Roll into a sheet approximately 1cm thick. Use to line six lightly greased ramekins, reserving enough to make lids.

Filling
500g beef rump steak
500g lamb rump
plain flour for dusting
salt and fine white pepper
1 carrot, peeled
1 stalk celery, peeled
1 medium onion, peeled
3 flat mushrooms, wiped clean with a damp cloth or paper towel
1 teaspoon each dried basil, oregano, tarragon
1 tablespoon Worcestershire sauce
1 teaspoon salt
1/2 teaspoon freshly ground black pepper
5 cups beef stock, preferably home-made

Trim the beef and lamb of all fat and sinew and cut into 1cm cubes. Season the flour with salt and white pepper and use it to dust the meat (tossing in a plastic bag or sieve works well). Grate the carrot and finely chop the celery, onion and mushrooms, from which you have removed the hard stalk ends. Combine well with the meats, dried herbs, Worcestershire sauce, salt and black pepper and spoon into the pastry-lined ramekins until each is nearly full. Half fill each with beef stock. Damp the edges of the pastry, roll out the remaining dough and form lids. Cover the ramekins and press the edges firmly to seal. Cover each ramekin with muslin or cotton cloth and tie securely with string. Place over simmering water in a steamer, cover and steam for 1½ hours. Prepare the sauce while the puddings are cooking.

Note: These puddings freeze well and can be reheated in a microwave. The oysters are best added at the last minute.

Sauce
2 red capsicums (peppers)
300ml demi-glace (reduced stock, available at good delicatessens), or unthickened gravy
2 tablespoons capers, rinsed and drained
30 black olives, destoned
1 tablespoon Worcestershire sauce

Remove and discard the stalk, seeds and ribs from the capsicums and grill until the skin blackens. Place in a paper bag until cool and remove the skin. Cut into thin strips. Heat the demi-glace or gravy and stir in one tablespoon of the capers, half the capsicum, ten of the olives and the Worcestershire sauce.

To serve
2 raw oysters per serving

Remove the puddings from the oven and unwrap. Cut a small slit in the top of each and push in two oysters. Place the ramekins on plates and spoon the sauce over the top. Garnish with the reserved olives, capsicum strips and capers.

Serves 6
Recomended wine:
Okahu Estate Ninety Mile Cabernet Sauvignon/Merlot

Recipe from Raewyn and Tony Lancaster

WAIPOUA LODGE, WAIPOUA FOREST, DARGAVILLE

City of Sails – and Cafés

Auckland

*A*uckland promotes itself as the City of Sails, a reference to the important part the sparkling harbour plays in the life of so many of its inhabitants.

But the country's largest city is also home to literally thousands of bars, cafés and restaurants. The mild climate means eating outdoors is a realistic alternative for most of the year, and residents and visitors use this advantage to the full.

The style is eclectic. As in any major city, chefs source their ingredients from around the country, but they place a major emphasis on local suppliers.

Auckland has more Polynesian inhabitants than anywhere else in the world, and one in seven of its residents comes from Asia. This exciting cultural mix has had a big effect on both its restaurants and its art.

Look at the recipes on the following pages. Turmeric and chillies are used to flavour farmed venison, local shellfish sit in a Thai-inspired broth, and fern fronds, a traditional delicacy for Maori, provide flavour accents on a couple of dishes.

A stroll through a selection of the city's many galleries will reveal that Maori, Pacific Islands and, to a lesser degree, Asian influences are also evident in the city's art.

Auckland is a great city, but its residents are always keen to enjoy a break in the nearby country. The Hauraki Gulf plays host to a plethora of islands, some accessible by commercial ferry. Most prominent is Waiheke, which in recent years has raised its profile with a series of startlingly good wines – the reds have been compared to the great clarets of France's Bordeaux region. Where there is good wine, there is bound to be good food, and Waiheke boasts several excellent restaurants, some with spectacular views.

Beaches are another popular weekend and holiday destination for Aucklanders, with a choice between the wild and rugged west coast and the rather more controlled – and considerably safer – east coast.

Auckland really has something for everyone.

The Viaduct Basin, home of the America's Cup 2003, with Auckland's Sky Tower behind.

Ascension Deerstalker's Pie

Harissa
100g dried chillies
6 cloves garlic
1 tablespoon caraway seeds
1 tablespoon coriander seeds
2 tablespoons olive oil
1 teaspoon cinnamon
1 teaspoon turmeric
1 teaspoon paprika
1 teaspoon black mustard seeds
1 tablespoon cumin powder

Soak the chillies in warm water for 5 minutes, then drain. Dry-fry the caraway and coriander seeds in a heavy frypan until fragrant. Place all the ingredients in a blender until smooth. (Harissa can be stored in the refrigerator for up to 3 months).

1kg diced cervena (shank ends, topside or rump)
olive oil
10 pickling onions
2 carrots
2 stalks celery
2 tablespoons soy bean oil
¹/₃ cup flour
300ml red wine (at Ascension, The Ascent Cabernet Sauvignon/Merlot/ Malbec is used)
1 litre beef stock, preferably home-made
sea salt and freshly ground black pepper
1kg kumara
2 large parsnips
2 tablespoons olive oil
filo pastry

Toss the cervena with harissa to taste and marinate overnight. The next morning, seal the meat in a hot pan, adding a little more olive oil if necessary, and put aside. Don't wash the pan.

Peel the onions and peel and roughly chop the carrots and celery stalks. Heat the soy bean oil in a large saucepan and cook the onions, carrots and celery until they soften a little. Add the flour, stir for a couple of minutes, then pour in enough wine to form a roux. Heat the stock and add slowly, stirring to prevent lumps from forming. Deglaze the pan in which the cervena was cooked with the remaining red wine and add to the vegetables, along with the meat. Season to taste. Bring to the boil and simmer on low heat for 1–1½ hours, or until the meat is very tender. Meanwhile, peel the kumara and parsnips and cut into 2cm chunks, drizzle with olive oil and roast in a 200°C oven until golden. Add to the pan for the last 30 minutes of cooking.

To complete and serve
Place the mixture in individual ceramic pie dishes and top with a single sheet of scrunched filo pastry. Bake in a 200°C oven until golden, and serve with rustic bread and a simple green salad for lunch, or mashed potatoes and winter greens at night.

Serves 8–10
Recommended wine:
The Ascent Cabernet Sauvignon/Merlot/Malbec

Recipe from
Michael Foxall

ASCENSION VINEYARD CAFE
MATAKANA

Above: Souzie Speerstra's The Red Boat, Waiheke Island *(acrylic on canvas) evokes memories of holidays relaxing at the water's edge. Souzie's work is vivid in colour and flowing in its form, as seen in the red boat bathing in summer sun at Enclosure Bay.*

Below: The tranquil harbour at Leigh, north of Auckland.

Peppered Ostrich Steaks
with truffled figs, port and basil

6 'pearl' ostrich steaks
4 large red onions
¹/₃ cup olive oil
1 cup balsamic vinegar
125g brown sugar
1 teaspoon sea salt
250ml tawny port (any good brand)
8 basil leaves
4 tablespoons crème fraîche
juice and rind of 1 lemon
1 cup self-raising flour
1 cup beer (any good brand)
2 teaspoons white sugar
1 teaspoon salt
sea salt
cracked black pepper
vegetable oil for deep-frying

Halve the ostrich steaks horizontally and remove any sinew. Peel the red onions and slice into thin rings. Reserve a quarter of the rings and put the others in a pan with most of the olive oil, balsamic vinegar, brown sugar and sea salt. Cook until the mixture forms a syrup.

Place the port and basil leaves, roughly torn, into a saucepan, bring to the boil and reduce by three-quarters, then strain. Keep warm. Mix the crème fraîche with the lemon juice and rind and refrigerate. Mix the flour, beer, sugar and salt to form a batter.

Season the ostrich steaks with sea salt and cracked black pepper, pressing into both sides. Heat a little olive oil in a heavy pan and cook the steaks for 1¹/₂ minutes on each side, or until well browned but still rare. Put in a warm place to rest for 10 minutes. Heat the vegetable oil, dip the reserved onion rings into the beer batter and deep-fry until golden. Drain on paper towels.

To complete and serve
6 figs
2 teaspoons truffle oil
salt and pepper

Halve the figs horizontally, drizzle with the oil and season. Grill, cut side up, for 30 seconds. Divide the caramelised onion among heated serving plates and top each with two pieces of ostrich. Dab with the lemon crème fraîche and top with the fig halves. Drizzle with the port reduction and garnish with the deep-fried onion rings.

Serves 6
Recommended wine:
Harrier Rise Cabernet Franc

Recipe from Nick Huffman
NICK'S WOOD FIRED GRILL
KUMEU

Above: The traditional art of tattooing, practised throughout the Pacific, is now widely accepted as a legitimate form of artistic expression for the tattooist and the wearer. This tuatara tattoo is an example of the work Inia Taylor does in his Grey Lynn studio.

Below: Wine maturing quietly in oak barrels at Matua Valley Wines, Waimauku, West Auckland.

Sushi

1kg short grain rice
25g salt
90g sugar
150ml rice vinegar

Wash the rice in a strainer until the water runs clear. Drain well and allow to stand for 30 minutes so the rice can absorb any moisture and become fluffy. Meanwhile, make sushi vinegar by stirring the salt and sugar into the vinegar until it dissolves.

Put the washed rice into a saucepan with 1400ml cold water and bring to the boil. Turn the heat down, cover and simmer for 11 minutes. Turn the heat up and boil for 1 minute more, then remove from the heat and allow to stand for a further 12 minutes. Leave covered through the whole process.

Transfer the rice to a wooden bowl and pour on the sushi vinegar at a rate of roughly four teaspoons for every cup of cooked rice. Mix by slicing with a rice paddle or flat wooden spoon, using a slashing rather than stirring motion to ensure the rice doesn't get 'mulched'. Allow to cool, cover with a damp cloth and refrigerate until required.

Rainbow Roll
2 eggs
salt and white pepper
1 tablespoon vegetable oil
3 king prawns, cooked and shelled
¹/₂ small cucumber
nori sheets (available at Asian food stores)
Sushi rice, prepared as above
3 slices smoked salmon

Mix the eggs with chopsticks or a fork. Season. Heat the oil in a small frypan and cook the eggs to make a thin omelette, turning once. Peel and deseed the cucumber and cut the flesh lengthwise into thin slices about 10cm long. Slice the prawns thinly lengthwise. Place a nori sheet on a sushi mat and spread with sushi rice. Roll carefully, using the mat as a guide. Place alternate slices of salmon, cucumber, prawn and omelette on a sheet of plastic food wrap ensuring they overlap. Place the nori roll at one end and use the

food wrap to help roll the slices around the nori roll as shown in the photograph. (The food wrap remains on the outside.) Wrap firmly in the plastic food wrap and refrigerate until needed.

Eel and Tofu Roll
¹/₂ carrot
3 fresh shiitake mushrooms
1 block tofu
30g piece raw white fish
2 teaspoons light soy sauce
1 teaspoon sugar
pinch salt
150g Japanese eel (available at Asian food stores)
1 teaspoon cornflour

Peel and grate the carrot. Slice the shiitake mushrooms as finely as possible. Place the tofu, fish, soy sauce, sugar and salt in a food processor and process until the mixture becomes a paste. Stir in the carrot and shiitake mushrooms. Spread the eel, skin-side up, and flatten slightly with the heel of your hand. Sprinkle with the cornflour and spread with the fish paste. Roll up and secure with a toothpick. Steam over simmering water for 15 minutes.

Eel Sauce
2 teaspoons light soya sauce
2 teaspoons mirin (Japanese sweet cooking sake)
2 teaspoons corn syrup
dash sugar

Mix all ingredients together and heat in a small saucepan.

To complete and serve
Arrange the Eel Rolls on plates and drizzle with the sauce. Slice the Rainbow Roll into 2cm discs, remove the plastic food wrap and place alongside.

Serves 4
Recommended wine:
Villa Maria Reserve Clifford Bay Sauvignon Blanc

Recipe from Yukio Suzuki

CAFE PACIFIQUE, CARLTON HOTEL, AUCKLAND

Above: Based in Grey Lynn, Phill Rooke talks of his work as 'pictorial storying'. Don't tern (top) and Kokakos are still about are two works from his '51 Series'. These polychrome acrylic wood reliefs are linked to the cultural environment of 1951 and encapsulate aspects of New Zealand's history as it relates to current issues.

Rocket Salad with Poached Pears,

Kikorangi blue cheese and caramelised walnuts

Poached Pears
5 medium–large poached pears
600ml water
200ml dry white wine
120g caster sugar
3 whole cloves
2 bay leaves
4 juniper berries
1 cinnamon stick
1 strip orange peel

These can be prepared 2–3 days in advance. Place the whole peeled and cored pears with the other ingredients in a large saucepan, bring to the boil and simmer for 15 minutes, or until just tender. Remove from heat, but leave the pears to cool in the liquid. Transfer the pears and liquid to a clean container and refrigerate until required.

Caramelised Walnuts
1 cup walnuts
1 cup water
³/₄ cup caster sugar
pinch salt

These can be prepared up to a day in advance. Bring the water and caster sugar to the boil in a saucepan. Continue to boil until the liquid caramelises, turning a golden amber colour. Remove from the heat. Add the salt, then the walnuts. Stir until the nuts are completely coated and the mixture starts to cool. Pour over a cooling rack placed on a steel tray to catch the caramel. Once cooled and crisp, remove from the rack, break up if necessary and place in an airtight container until required.

To complete and serve
250g rocket
200g Kapiti Kikorangi blue (or other cheese)
1¹/₂ tablespoons balsamic vinegar
2 tablespoons olive oil
pinch sea salt
pinch pepper

Wash and dry the rocket leaves and place in a large bowl. Cut the cheese into fine dice and add. Remove the pears from the syrup and cut into even slices. Add to the salad mix. Add the caramelised walnuts. Add the balsamic vinegar and oil, season to taste and toss carefully. Distribute among six serving bowls.

Serves 6
Recommended wine:
Kumeu River Chardonnay

Recipe from Alistair Parker
METROPOLE, AUCKLAND

Below: Flower Pendant *by Tania Patterson is made of sterling silver and paduk (African wood). Tania is a contemporary jeweller who works from her Newton studio. Her jewellery is based on seed and plant forms with an element of surprise introduced by the use of contrasting colour and industrial materials.*

Rack of Hawke's Bay Lamb
with a herb and parmesan crust

4 x 180g lamb racks
4 tablespoons olive oil
salt and pepper
³/₄ cup grated parmesan
³/₄ cup breadcrumbs
1 bunch chervil
1 small bunch Italian flatleaf parsley
4 tablespoons unsalted butter
20 baby leeks
3 cloves garlic
1 sprig thyme
3 tablespoons olive oil
3 cups chicken stock
4–6 tomatoes
1 red onion
small bunch basil
2 cups couscous
1 tablespoon butter
2 tablespoons white wine vinegar
6 tablespoons extra virgin olive oil
4 servings rocket leaves
4 tablespoons red wine jus (stock or
unthickened gravy reduced with red wine)

Ask the butcher to 'French trim' the lamb racks and remove excess fat. Heat two tablespoons of olive oil in a heavy frypan and seal the racks. Season and put aside. Place the parmesan, breadcrumbs, chervil, parsley and butter into a blender and process until well mixed. Season to taste, then smear the coating over the backs of the lamb racks. Roast in a 180°C oven for approximately 12–15 minutes, or until medium-rare.

Meanwhile, trim the baby leeks, discarding most of the green tops. Peel and finely chop the garlic. Strip the leaves from the thyme sprig and chop. Heat two tablespoons of olive oil in a heavy frypan and toss the leeks with the garlic and thyme until slightly coloured. Add four tablespoons of chicken stock, season and bring to the boil, then braise for 8–10 minutes in a 180°C oven.

Cut a shallow cross in the stem end of each tomato and put them into boiling water for 20 seconds. Plunge into cold water, then peel and deseed. Cut into quarters and grill very lightly. Cut into 'petals' and use to line four small moulds.

Peel and thinly slice the red onion and sweat with torn basil leaves in the remaining olive oil until it softens and turns slightly golden. Add the couscous and stir. Boil the remaining chicken stock with a little butter and pour over the couscous. Leave in a warm place until the stock is absorbed, then push the mixture firmly into the tomato-lined moulds. Shake the vinegar and olive oil together in a screwtop jar, season and use it to dress the rocket leaves.

To complete and serve

Turn the couscous moulds out onto heated serving plates. Cut each lamb rack into two pieces and arrange to suit, along with the baby leeks and rocket salad. Briefly heat the red wine jus and drizzle around the edge.

Serves 4

Recommended wine:

La Strada Marlborough Pinot Noir

Recipe from Stephen Thompson

PARTINGTON'S, SHERATON HOTEL AND TOWERS AUCKLAND

Right: This is the view of Auckland enjoyed by visitors arriving in cruise ships, and also by the thousands of workers who commute by ferry from the North Shore and outlying islands. The skyline is dominated by the needle-like Sky Tower. At 328m, it is the tallest tower in the Southern Hemisphere.

Controversial when it was built, this impressive example of modern engineering is now accepted by the majority of citysiders as a worthwhile addition to the mélange of high-rise buildings. It offers adventure seekers the opportunity to experience a world first, Sky Jump, a 192m vertical fall on a cable.

On weekends and summer evenings the harbour in the foreground is crowded with pleasure boats seemingly intent on proving that Auckland really is the 'City of Sails'.

Fresh Fish
with green vegetable spring rolls in Thai basil broth

Spring Rolls
1 green capsicum (pepper)
1 leek
1 courgette (zucchini)
1 white onion
2 spring onions
2 heads bok choy
2 tablespoons vegetable oil
sea salt and white pepper
4 spring roll pastries
1 egg yolk

Remove and discard the stalk, ribs and seeds from the capsicum, the roots and green parts of the leek and spring onions, and the ends of the courgette. Thinly slice all the vegetables and sweat for 2–3 minutes in the oil. Season to taste, then spread onto a tray to cool. Divide into four even piles and wrap each one in a spring roll pastry, forming a tidy cylinder. Brush the join with egg yolk to seal, and refrigerate until needed.

Thai Basil Broth
1cm piece fresh ginger
4 cloves garlic
1 coriander root
rind of 1 orange
3 tablespoons Japanese soy sauce
4 teaspoons fish sauce
4 teaspoons mirin (Japanese cooking sake)
2 teaspoons sake

Peel the ginger and garlic and trim the coriander root. Place with all other ingredients in a saucepan and add $1^3/_4$ cups water. Heat to a slow simmer, cook for 5 minutes then allow to cool, covered, for 2 hours. Pass through a fine sieve, keeping the broth and discarding the solid ingredients.

To complete and serve
200g baby clams, pipi or tuatua
2 heads bok choy
handful Thai basil
vegetable oil for pan-frying and deep-frying
4 x 150g fillets fresh firm-fleshed fish
salt and pepper

Soak the shellfish in several changes of water to rid them of sand. Bring the Thai Basil Broth to the boil. Lower the heat, add the shellfish, cover and cook at a very low simmer just until they open. Cut the bok choy in half lengthwise, roughly tear the Thai basil leaves and add both to the broth for the last few seconds of cooking. Heat a little oil in a heavy frypan, season the fish and seal on both sides, then transfer to a 220°C oven for 6–8 minutes. Heat the remaining oil in a deep fryer and cook the spring rolls until crisp and golden brown. Drain on paper towels. The objective is for all three component parts of the dish to be cooked at the same time.

To serve, place the broth with the clams and bok choy in heated deep bowls, check the seasoning, then remove the fish from the oven and place on top. Season the spring rolls, cut on an angle and arrange on top of the fish.

Serves 4
Recommended wine:
Matakana Estate Chardonnay

Recipe from Sean Armstrong

O'CONNELL STREET BISTRO
AUCKLAND

Horopito Beef
with avocado mash and piko piko

4 x 200g beef eye fillet steaks
2 tablespoons Horopito rub (available at good delicatessens)
³/₄ cup avocado oil
4–6 potatoes
salt and pepper

Trim the steaks, removing all fat and skin. Stir a teaspoon of the Horopito rub into four tablespoons of the avocado oil and rub into the steaks. Leave to marinate for at least 10 minutes. Combine the remaining rub with a quarter cup of avocado oil and leave in a warm place to combine the flavours.

Peel the potatoes and cut into large dice. Place in salted water, bring to the boil and cook for 10 minutes, or until soft. Drain and shake over low heat to dry. Mash until smooth, then drizzle in enough avocado oil to make a smooth mash. Season to taste and keep warm.

To complete and serve
12 piko piko (fern fronds, available from some delicatessens)
2–3 kumara
vegetable oil for deep-frying
¹/₃ cup red wine
¹/₂ cup liquid beef stock (available from some supermarkets)
2 tablespoons butter, chilled

Cook the piko piko in boiling salted water for 2–3 minutes, or until tender. Drain and keep warm. Peel the kumara and cut into thin chips (about ¹/₂ cm-square). Wash and pat dry, then deep-fry in the oil until golden. Drain on paper towels and keep warm. Put two tablespoons of the oil into a heavy frypan and sear the steaks for a few minutes on each side. They should be rare or medium-rare. Remove to a warm place and add the red wine and beef stock to the pan, stirring in all the brown bits. Reduce by one-third and keep warm. To serve, place a pile of mashed potatoes on each heated plate and arrange the steaks on top. Whisk the

butter into the wine reduction sauce, working just off the heat, and pour over the top. Drizzle the reserved Horopito-infused avocado oil around the edge and top with the kumara chips. Garnish with the piko piko.

Serves 4
Recommended wine:
Te Mata Estate Hawke's Bay Cabernet Sauvignon/Merlot

Recipe from Mike Daly
THE CAFE, HYATT REGENCY AUCKLAND

Left: Oriori *(top) and* Ahuru Mowai *(acrylic on board), by Gabrielle Belz, are from a series of works entitled 'Ka Tu Te Rito' and refer to an ongoing connectedness with our beginnings and future, the inherent qualities that make us who we are. The series depicts the nurturing of strengths that enable us to stand tall in the temporal and spiritual landscape we move through. Gabrielle is of Ngapuhi and Te Atiawa descent and lives in Auckland.*

Right: The Comet *by Bill Hayes is bronze patinated in classic verdigris. Bill's work delves into the personal and familiar realms and draws from an interest in surfaces, direction, interior space and nature.*

Lamb Fillets on Roasted Vegetables
with basil pesto

1kg lamb fillets
2 cups olive oil
3 sprigs rosemary
salt and pepper to taste
2kg ripe but firm tomatoes
1kg red onions
4 tablespoons balsamic vinegar
2 tablespoons brown sugar
1 cup basil leaves
50g pine nuts
50g freshly grated parmesan
2 spring onions
1kg golden kumara
1kg red kumara
1kg potatoes
1 pumpkin
piko piko fern fronds

Trim the lamb fillets and put them in a shallow dish with one cup of the olive oil and the fresh rosemary. Season lightly then refrigerate for 24 hours.

Core the tomatoes, cut into wedges and place in a bowl. Thinly slice one red onion and add, then stir in half a cup of olive oil, the balsamic vinegar, brown sugar and a little salt and pepper. Refrigerate.

Place the basil leaves, remaining olive oil, pine nuts and parmesan in a blender, food processor or mortar and pestle and process until smooth, but still a little chunky. Place in a screwtop jar and refrigerate. This is pesto, and is a useful ingredient to have on hand.

Trim the spring onions, discarding most of the green ends, and peel the kumara, potatoes, remaining onions and pumpkin. Cut into wedges, scatter over an oven tray and sprinkle with olive oil. Season with salt and pepper and roast in a 200°C oven for 45 minutes, or until cooked and golden brown.

To complete and serve
Pan-fry the lamb fillets in a little of their marinating oil for 2 minutes, turning regularly, or until just cooked but still quite pink. Rest them for 5 minutes on a warm plate while you distribute the roasted vegetables between the heated serving plates. Place the fillets on top, whole or sliced, and dab with basil pesto. Garnish with the marinated tomatoes and piko piko.

Serves 6–8
Recommended wine:
Matakana Estate
Merlot/Cabernet Sauvignon

Recipe from Bridgette Davis
NUMBER 5 WINE BISTRO
AUCKLAND

Above: Originally from Holland, Helena Blair describes Waiheke as her favourite haven. The vineyard in Vineyard at Stony Batter *(acrylic on canvas) overlooks Hooks Bay at the northern end of the island. Beyond the hills one can explore huge stone formations and old bunkers, remnants of wartime fortifications.*

The flax bush, or harakeke, is an iconic New Zealand plant much loved by native birds. This view looking north along spectacular Muriwai Beach was taken from the gannet colony, well known to ornithologists around the world.

Pan-seared Salmon
on sweet paprika couscous

12 spears asparagus
800g fresh salmon fillet (4 x 200g servings)
2 tablespoons canola oil
1 chorizo (spicy Spanish sausage)
1 tablespoon extra virgin olive oil
1 teaspoon red wine vinegar
salt and freshly ground white pepper
4 cups mixed greens and shoots (mesclun,
watercress, snow pea shoots, alfalfa,
chickweed, rocket, mustard, cress, etc)

Peel the asparagus spears from a point about 1cm below the start of the flower heads. Snap off the tough bases and trim. Brush with a little olive oil, season and cook on a barbecue or ridged grill pan. Heat the canola oil in a heavy pan and sear the salmon on one side until crisp and golden, turn, cook for a further few seconds then remove and keep warm. Cut the chorizo sausage into angled chunks and cook in the same pan.

Make a dressing from the extra virgin olive oil and red wine vinegar, season to taste then use it to toss the greens.

To complete and serve
Sweet Paprika Couscous (see page 188)

Distribute the couscous among the serving bowls and top with the salmon, chorizo and asparagus. Season to taste and arrange the salad carefully on top.

Serves 4
Recommended wine:
Babich Reserve Syrah, or Matua
Judd Estate Chardonnay

Recipe from Geoffrey Scott

WHITE RESTAURANT, HILTON
HOTEL, AUCKLAND

Right: Auckland's Princes Wharf plays
host to a series of cruise ships through
the summer months, providing constant
entertainment for residents of the
apartment block and the plush Hilton
Hotel, both built right on the wharf.

Vegetable Stacks

Kumara Rosti
1 large gold kumara
2 tablespoons olive oil (the Vista-Vitae chef uses Waiheke Wild)
salt and pepper
3 tablespoons vegetable oil

Peel and grate the kumara. Squeeze out excess moisture. Mix the kumara with the olive oil and seasoning. Heat the vegetable oil in a heavy frypan and fry in spoonfuls over moderate heat, making each rosti the size of the flat mushrooms (below). Drain on paper towels then transfer to a tray lined with baking paper. There should be eight to twelve. (The rosti can be made 4–5 hours in advance).

Vegetables
1 red capsicum (pepper)
1 yellow capsicum (pepper)
8 large flat mushrooms
6 sprigs fresh rosemary
2 cloves garlic
4 tablespoons extra virgin olive oil
1 tablespoon balsamic vinegar

Discard the stems, seeds and ribs from the capsicums and cut each into four flat pieces. Trim the mushroom stalks and wipe the caps clean with a damp paper towel. Strip the rosemary leaves from two of the stalks and chop. Peel and finely chop the garlic. Combine all ingredients and turn gently to get an even covering of oil and vinegar. Place the capsicums and mushrooms in a heavy roasting dish and cook for 10 minutes in a 200°C oven, on fan-bake if possible. Place the pre-cooked Kumara Rosti on a separate tray and add for the last 5 minutes of cooking time.

To complete and serve
Place one rosti on each heated serving plate and top with a mushroom. Add a piece each of red and yellow capsicum and keep alternating until everything is used up. Drizzle with the cooking juices, plus a little extra olive oil and balsamic vinegar if you like. Garnish with a sprig of rosemary.

Serves 4
Recommended wine:
Obsidian Waiheke Island
Cabernet Sauvignon/Merlot

Recipe from Susan Story

VISTA-VITAE
WAIHEKE

Top left: Waiheke's Vista-Vitae Cooking School

Top right: Oneroa and the islands of the Hauraki Gulf, as seen from Vista-Vitae.

Above: This work, Paakahukahu (harakeke, kanuka, kiekie and Torere stones), is one in a series of panels woven by Waiheke Island artist/weaver, Mex Hennebry. The name of this panel means 'strength'. Mex's work is produced in mixed media using only natural materials and is often based on concepts of body, mind and spirit, or birth, life and death.

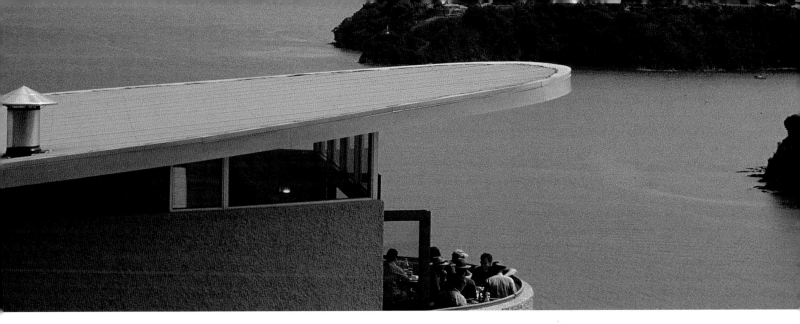

Seared Encrusted Tuna
with roast capsicum

Anchovy Aïoli
1 egg
2 tablespoons wholegrain mustard
1 tablespoon balsamic vinegar
3 good quality anchovy fillets
2 tablespoons capers
2 cloves garlic
salt and pepper to taste
2 cups soy bean oil

Place all ingredients except the oil in a food processor or blender and process until well blended. Drizzle in the oil, drop by drop at first, then in a thin stream. The mixture should be thick and creamy. Put aside.

Infused Oil
1 ¹/₂ cups soy bean oil
2 teaspoons ground turmeric
2 teaspoons mustard seeds
2 teaspoons ground coriander
2 teaspoons cumin

Heat two tablespoons of the soy bean oil in a saucepan and heat the spices until they are fragrant. Add the remaining oil and continue cooking over low heat for approximately 10 minutes. Allow to rest until the spices have sunk to the bottom and the oil is no longer cloudy.

6 red capsicums (peppers)
16 baby new potatoes
¹/₂ cup balsamic vinegar
3 limes
2 tablespoons caster sugar

Cook the capsicums whole on a heated ridged grill pan or over a gas flame, turning frequently, until blistered and blackened. Remove the skin, stems and seeds but leave the shape as original as possible. Scrub the potatoes, place in salted water and bring to the boil. Reduce the heat and simmer until almost cooked. Cut in half and put aside. Place the balsamic vinegar in a saucepan and cook until reduced to approximately three tablespoons. It should be quite thick. Cut the limes in half and dip the cut side into the caster sugar. Caramelise on the ridged grill pan.

To complete and serve
4 tablespoons olive oil
2 tablespoons clarified butter (see Note)
2 sprigs marjoram
salt and pepper to taste
3 tablespoons tougarasi (Japanese seven-spice mix, available at Asian food stores)
4 tablespoons black sesame seeds
4 tablespoons white sesame seeds
6 thick tuna steaks, 250–300g each
2 tablespoons olive oil

Heat two tablespoons of olive oil with the clarified butter in a heavy frypan and cook the potatoes until golden. Chop the marjoram leaves and scatter over the top. Season to taste. Combine tougarasi and sesame seeds and use the mixture to coat each side of the tuna steaks, pressing it well into the surface. Heat the remaining olive oil and sear the steaks for 45–60 seconds on each side. Place in a warm place to rest.

To serve, spoon a little Anchovy Aïoli onto each heated serving plate, place a roasted capsicum on top, then arrange the tuna steaks, potatoes and caramelised lime to suit. Drizzle with Infused Oil and balsamic reduction. The dish in the photograph also features blanched broccolini, and is garnished with Thai basil and Chinese chives.

Note: To clarify butter, heat in a small saucepan, skim froth from the top as it forms, and carefully tip the clear butter off the sediment at the bottom.

Serves 6
Recommended wine:
Te Whau Waiheke Island Chardonnay

Recipe from Kate McMillan

TE WHAU VINEYARD, WAIHEKE

Top left: Keeping marauding birds away from bunches of ripening grapes is a constant battle for viticulturists. Gas guns, programmed to fire at regular intervals, kites, scarecrows and coloured cloth tied to the trellising wires have some effect, but to be absolutely sure of keeping the crop intact the grower must net the vines. It's not infallible – occasionally a bird will get under the net and wreak havoc, but it is a better system than any other.

Top right: The spectacularly situated Te Whau restaurant.

Sugar-cured Tuna
with angel hair pasta and black olive dressing

2 teaspoons grated orange zest
2 teaspoons grated lemon zest
¹/₄ cup sea salt
¹/₂ cup sugar
1 teaspoon cracked black pepper
300g tuna loin
1 tablespoon olive oil

Mix the orange and lemon zests, salt, sugar and pepper together in a bowl. Add the tuna, turning to ensure good coverage. Marinate for 4 hours. Rinse the tuna thoroughly under running water and pat dry with paper towels. Heat the oil in a non-stick frypan and sear the tuna for a few seconds on all sides. It should be evenly coloured on the surface but still raw. Refrigerate.

Black Olive Dressing
4–6 sun-dried tomatoes
8 black olives
2 sprigs fresh thyme
1 sprig fresh rosemary
3 tablespoons balsamic vinegar
¹/₃ cup olive oil
salt and pepper to taste

Thinly slice the sun-dried tomatoes, deseed the olives and finely chop, strip the leaves from the thyme and rosemary and finely chop both. Whisk all ingredients together and season to taste. Put aside.

Pasta
enough angel hair pasta or thin Chinese egg noodles to yield 1 cup, cooked
3 sun-dried tomatoes
2 tablespoons watercress leaves

Cook the pasta according to the directions on the packet. Thinly slice the sun-dried tomatoes and toss with the pasta and leaves.

Salsa Verde
1 slice dryish white bread, such as ciabatta, crusts removed
2 tablespoons olive oil, plus more if required
1 garlic clove
2 anchovies
¹/₄ green capsicum (pepper)
2 tablespoons watercress leaves
3 tablespoons Italian flatleaf parsley leaves
1 tablespoon capers
juice of ¹/₂ small lemon (about 2 teaspoons)
salt to taste

Tear the bread into pieces and soak in two tablespoons of the olive oil. Peel the garlic. Remove and discard ribs and seeds from the capsicum. Place all ingredients in a blender or food processor and blend to form a thick sauce, adding more olive oil if necessary.

To complete and serve
4 tablespoons watercress leaves

Toss the Pasta with some of the dressing and distribute among the serving plates. Thinly slice the tuna and arrange around the pasta. Dab a little Salsa Verde on each slice. Drizzle extra dressing around the plate and garnish with the watercress leaves.

Serves 4
Recommended wine:
Huntaway Pinot Gris

Recipe from Richard Harris
SOUL BAR AND BISTRO
AUCKLAND

Top: In a few short years Auckland's Viaduct Basin has become a buzzing mecca for wine and food enthusiasts. Restaurants edging the water cater for every taste — and every pocket. Naturally, seafood features strongly, but there's plenty to please dedicated carnivores.

Far right: America's Cup fever attracts pleasure seekers from around the world.

Bubbly Surf, Boiling Mud

Coromandel and Bay of Plenty

*O*f all the regions featured in this book, the strip along the North Island's East Coast offers the most geographic variation.

For many years, logging and mining were the major activities in the bush-clad hills of Coromandel, and trampers still stumble across the rusted detritus of this semi-industrial past.

Nowadays, the region is better known as a haven for artists and craftspeople. The local clay takes kindly to the kiln, and many thousands of New Zealand homes give pride of place to pots or artworks picked up during a Coromandel holiday.

The hills are home to wild pigs and smaller game animals that draw hunters from around the country. On the coast, white-sand beaches attract young people in droves.

Head inland and you will soon be in the 'thermal wonderland' of Rotorua. This is the mecca for tourists from around the world, many of whom try food cooked in a hangi, or Maori earth-oven, while they are there. The food isn't all traditional – one entire street is devoted to restaurants and cafés serving an eclectic mix of dishes best described as 'modern New Zealand'.

Nearby is Tauranga, an immaculately maintained city known for its popularity with retirees, and Mt Maunganui, where a wide, sandy beach and predictable waves are a great attraction for surfers and holidaymakers.

The diversity of the landscape makes it difficult to pin down specifically local food styles, but there are plenty of sub-regional specialities. Shellfish reigns supreme in the Coromandel, both in restaurants and at home – pipi and tuatua, both in the clam family, are easily obtainable on the many beaches along the coast, and New Zealand's indigenous mussels are farmed in the shallows.

Wine is made in the Coromandel, but in tiny quantities and mostly from grapes grown outside the area. A couple of wineries have made the Tauranga district their home, but the grapes are sourced in other parts of the country. The nearest serious wine regions are further down the coast at Gisborne and Hawke's Bay.

From the summit of Mt Maunganui looking south along Ocean Beach.

Grilled Fish on Spicy Salad

Spicy Dressing
5 fresh chillies
5 cloves garlic, peeled
3 spring onions
5 tablespoons brown sugar
2 tablespoons rice wine vinegar
¼ cup fresh lemon or lime juice
¼ cup fish sauce (available at Asian food stores)
¼ cup vegetable oil

Deseed and finely chop the chillies. Finely chop the garlic and spring onions. Place with all other ingredients in a screwtop jar and shake vigorously until well blended.

Potato Base
4–6 potatoes, depending on size
3–4 tablespoons butter
salt and freshly ground pepper to taste

Peel and thinly slice the potatoes and place on an oven tray. Melt the butter and brush or drizzle some over the top, reserving the rest, then season. Cook in a 180°C oven for 10–15 minutes, or until they begin to turn crispy.

To complete and serve
4 x 150g fillets fresh firm-fleshed fish, skinned and boned
salt and freshly ground pepper
a good mixture of salad leaves
grated zest of 1 orange
3 lemons or limes, cut into wedges

Place the fish fillets on an oven tray, brush with the reserved melted butter and season. Bake in a 180°C oven until done to your liking, and to suit the type of fish. It can be cooked at the same time as the potatoes, but be aware that species like hapuku and tuna are best served rare or medium-rare, and other types will require little more than 4–5 minutes. While the fish and potatoes are cooking, toss the salad leaves with the spicy dressing. To assemble the dish, put the potatoes on heated serving plates and top with the salad leaves. Place the fish fillets on top and garnish with the orange zest and lemon or lime wedges.

Note: At Peppertree, the fish is topped with a generous dollop of garlic mayonnaise (aïoli). You can buy it, but you will achieve a better flavour if you make your own. Mix finely chopped garlic, roasted first if you prefer to soften the flavour, with mayonnaise made by drizzling oil, initially drop by drop and then in a thin stream, into well-whisked egg yolks. If it separates, whisk the turned mixture into a freshly whisked egg yolk, then continue adding the oil.

Serves 4
Recommended wine:
Brick Bay Matakana Pinot Gris

Recipe from Grant Allen
PEPPERTREE RESTAURANT
COROMANDEL

Above: An avid recycler, Dave Roy created Green Lagoon *using artificial rock from the set of* Lord of the Rings *(for which he assisted in the set design), paua, aluminium, stainless steel, rimu, corrugated iron and paint.*

Left: A lone surfer tests the waves at deserted Opito Bay, on the Coromandel Peninsula north of Whitianga.

Snapper and Scallop Roulade
with potato and smoked paprika salad

Potato and Smoked Paprika Salad
1 rasher bacon
1 medium potato per serving
1 large canned artichoke
4 capers
1 gherkin
1 tablespoon commercial mayonnaise
$^1/_2$ teaspoon smoked paprika
salt and freshly ground black pepper to taste

Grill the bacon until crisp, allow to cool then crumble into small pieces. Peel and cook the potato, leaving it slightly firm, then dice. Chop the artichoke and capers finely. Roughly dice the gherkin. Combine all ingredients, taking care not to break up the potato cubes.

Scallop Mousse
100g scallops
$^1/_2$ teaspoon fish sauce (available at Asian food stores)
1 egg white
40ml cream
salt and white pepper to taste

Remove roe from half the scallops and put aside with the whole scallops. Place the roeless scallops in a blender with the fish sauce and egg white and process until very smooth. Add the cream, process briefly and season to taste.

To complete and serve:
150g thin snapper fillet
salt and pepper
4 nori sheets (available at Asian food stores)
60g sliced smoked salmon (any good commercial brand)

Flatten or cut the snapper fillet slightly if necessary to make it thin and flexible. Season to taste. Place a sheet of nori on a board, spread the reserved scallops and extra roes over the top and roll into a cylinder. Place another sheet of nori on the board and cover with smoked

salmon slices. Roll this around the first cylinder. Repeat the process with the scallop mousse, then the snapper fillet. Finally, wrap the entire roulade in foil, twist the ends and cook in a 180°C oven for 12–15 minutes. Remove the foil and cut into 1cm slices. Arrange on a serving plate with the potato salad alongside.

Serves 1
Recommended wine:
Cooper's Creek Hawke's Bay Riesling
Recipe from Harry Williams

THE FIREPLACE
WHITIANGA

Below: Moko, *by Todd Couper, is a contemporary kauri carving decorated with paint, depicting a stylised male face in profile with a simplified version of the traditional moko or facial tattoo. Todd is of Ngati Kahungunu descent and now lives in Rotorua, where he sculpts and carves wood in traditional and contemporary styles.*

Rhubarb Clafoutis
with yoghurt

1 tablespoon butter mixed with
3 teaspoons sugar
5 eggs
1 vanilla pod
250g sugar
¹/₂ cup plain flour
pinch salt
1 cup cream
1 cup whole-cream milk
grated zest of 1 orange
1–2 tablespoons Galliano liqueur
8 stalks rhubarb
Cyclops organic yoghurt for serving

Rub the inside of a baking dish with the butter and sugar mixture. Sift the flour. Beat the eggs with the vanilla pod in a cake mixer until frothy. Add the sugar, flour, salt, cream, milk, orange zest and Galliano. Mix until well blended (about 2 minutes) and put aside.

Peel the rhubarb and cut into small batons. Lay out on the baking tray and pour the liquid mixture over the top. Bake in a 180°C oven until golden-brown and set (about 40 minutes). Place on a rack to cool slightly before serving.

Serves 6–8
Recommended wine:
Lawson's Dry Hills Late Harvest

Recipe from Rick Lowe and
Annie Butcher

Somerset Cottage
Tauranga

Right: Coromandel's Granite Wharf is a local landmark.

Far Right: Sydney-born Tom Mutch lives and works in Kuaotunu, Coromandel Peninsula. His oil paintings, silk screens and sculptures have allegorical themes. The Pathway (oil on board) is set in his garden and features red hot pokers and lacebark trees.

Red Curried Fish
with lime, coconut and coriander

*1 teaspoon fennel seeds, dry-fried
until fragrant*
6 cloves garlic, peeled and chopped
6cm piece fresh ginger, peeled and chopped
3 hot red chillies (deseed if you prefer)
6 kaffir lime leaves
2 teaspoons shrimp paste
100ml sesame oil
2 medium red onions, finely chopped
1.2kg fish fillets, cut into 2 pieces
600ml unsweetened coconut milk
*4 tablespoons fish sauce (available at
Asian food stores)*

Put the first six ingredients into a food processor with half the sesame oil and purée to a fine paste. Heat the remaining oil in a heavy saucepan and fry the onion for 2 minutes over high heat, stirring well to prevent it from burning. Add the fish pieces and fry for 1 minute, turning to seal all over. Remove the onions and fish and put aside. Reheat the saucepan and add the puréed paste. Fry for 1 minute, stirring well, then return the fish and onion to the pan. Add the coconut milk and bring to a fast simmer. Add the fish sauce and cook for 5 minutes, or until the fish is done. Meanwhile, make the Coriander Sauce (see page 189).

To complete and serve
Place the fish curry in heated bowls and spoon the sauce over the top.

Serves 6

Recomended wine:

*Mills Reef Reserve
Gewürztraminer*

Recipe from Kate Goodman

WHARF ST RESTAURANT
TAURANGA

Far right: This large stone sculpture in Spring Street, Tauranga, is by the late Tuti Tikaokao. It depicts the legend of Taurikura, a young girl who was transformed into a taniwha (a mythical, magical, dragon-like being).

Chargrilled Hapuku
with peppered lentils, kina cream and cress pesto

Cress Pesto
¹/₂ cup pine nuts
¹/₂ cup pumpkin seeds
1 packed cup fresh watercress
1 packed cup fresh basil
2 cloves garlic
¹/₄ cup avocado oil
1 tablespoon grated parmesan
sea salt and freshly ground black
pepper to taste

Dry-fry or grill the pine nuts and pumpkin seeds until fragrant. Pulse the watercress, basil and garlic in a food processor, then add the oil, parmesan, pine nuts and pumpkin seeds, aiming for a coarse texture. Season to taste.

Kina Cream
1 cup seafood stock (see Note)
1 cup cream
1 cup dry white wine (the Astrolabe kitchen uses Mills Reef Chardonnay)
200g fresh kina roe, finely chopped
sea salt and freshly ground black
pepper to taste

Bring the stock, cream and wine to the boil. Simmer and reduce by half. Add the kina roe to the liquid and whisk until reasonably smooth. Season to taste.

Peppered Lentils
100g puy lentils

Pick over the lentils, discarding any 'debris', and rinse. Place in a saucepan, cover with cold water, bring to the boil and simmer until just cooked (about 20 minutes). Drain.

Above right: Michael Smither is an artist, observer, composer, ecologist and teacher who lives in Otama, Coromandel Peninsula, and has a passion for paint. His Whitianga Composition *(oil-alkyd on board) is a spontaneous, fresh outdoor study.*

Right: Mt Maunganui, a popular summer playground and retirement destination.

To complete and serve
4 x 170g hapuku fillet per serving
2 tablespoons olive oil
sea salt and black pepper to taste
fresh watercress
lemon wedges

Pat the fillets dry and brush with oil. Pan-fry for 1 minute on each side then place in a 180°C oven for 3–4 minutes. The fish is perfectly cooked when it is still slightly pink in the middle. Season with sea salt and pepper and keep warm. Toss the Peppered Lentils with the Kina Cream and a generous amount of freshly ground black pepper and place on heated plates. Top with a hapuku fillet and drizzle with the Cress Pesto. Garnish with the watercress sprigs and lemon wedges.

Note: To make seafood stock, gently simmer fish frames and any vegetable offcuts and herbs you have on hand for 20 minutes. Strain carefully.

Serves 4
Recommended wine:
Mills Reef Hawke's Bay
Chardonnay 2000

Recipe from Mark Zephyr-Peterson
ASTROLABE CAFE AND BAR
MT MAUNGANUI

Below: Heather Hobbs's Moth Brooch is made from paua shell, sterling silver and goat horn. Heather describes herself as a mixed media craftsperson but primarily a carver, and uses natural materials with inlays to give colour and texture. Most of her pieces are for body adornment and evolve from natural forms. She works, mothers, and gardens with her husband Alan beside the Ohau Channel in the Bay of Plenty.

Baked Salmon
with udon noodles and salsa

Udon Mixture
200g fresh udon noodles
2 preserved lemons (available at good delicatessens)
1 tablespoon chopped fresh coriander
1 tablespoon chopped fresh Italian flatleaf parsley
6 olives, mixed black and green

Cook the noodles according to the directions on the packet (in most cases, boiling water is poured over them, left for 5 minutes then drained off). Thinly slice the lemons, then add them and the herbs to the drained noodles. Toss with the olives, then refrigerate for at least 2 hours.

Salsa
1 fully ripe tomato
$^1/_4$ cucumber
$^1/_2$ small red onion
1 small red, yellow or orange capsicum (pepper)
1 tablespoon white wine vinegar
3 tablespoons extra virgin olive oil
salt and cracked black pepper to taste

Dice the tomato, discarding the seeds and watery insides. Dice the cucumber, discarding the seeds if they are very watery. Peel and dice the red onion. Remove and discard the stem, seeds and white ribs from the capsicum and dice the flesh. Toss the mixture with the vinegar and olive oil, season to taste and refrigerate, but allow to reach room temperature before serving.

Baked Salmon
200g salmon fillet (skin on or off, as you prefer)
1 lemon
salt and cracked black pepper to taste
2 tablespoons olive oil

Remove any pin bones from the salmon with tweezers or needle-nosed pliers. Squeeze lemon juice over the top and season. Heat the oil, sear the salmon and

finish in a 180°C oven. It should be served medium-rare at most, so it will be cooked in less than 5 minutes. Meanwhile, toss the Udon Mixture with a little olive oil in a frypan, stirring continuously to prevent it from sticking. Arrange on a heated plate, place the salmon fillet on top and finish with the Salsa.

Serves 1
(Multiply the salmon and udon as necessary, but the salsa should do for two or three servings)

Recommended wine:
Church Road Cuve Series
Sauvignon Blanc

Recipe from Heinz Tell
FREOS CAFE, ROTORUA

Above: Waitukei, *by artist and master carver Lyonel Grant (Ngati Pikiao, Te Arawa), is in the Rotorua Museum garden. This cast bronze sculpture created over a two-year period 'attests to the contribution each local person, male or female, regardless of age has made to the fabric of our society'.*

Top left: A classic sunset near Matamata.

Pistachio-crusted Loin of Lamb

with lemon risotto cake and a Mediterranean vegetable salad

Risotto Cake

¼ cup butter
1 onion
1 cup arborio rice
4 cups (approximately) chicken stock, ideally home-made
grated zest of 1 lemon
¾ cup grated parmesan cheese
2 eggs

Melt the butter in a heavy-based saucepan and pan-fry the onion until soft but not coloured. Add the rice, unwashed (the starch gives the risotto its texture) and stir to mix. Pour in the stock ladle by ladle, letting the rice absorb it each time. The mixture should move in slow waves when the pan is tipped. When the rice is cooked but is still just firm to bite into (20–25 minutes, depending on the brand) stir in the lemon zest and parmesan cheese. Allow to cool slightly, then stir in the eggs. Spread about 2cm thick on a tray and refrigerate overnight.

Crust

1 cup fresh breadcrumbs
1 cup pistachio nuts
salt and pepper to taste

Blend the breadcrumbs and nuts in a food processor. Season to taste.

Mediterranean Vegetable Salad

3 courgettes (zucchini)
1 eggplant (aubergine)
3 red, yellow or orange capsicums (peppers), or 1 of each colour
1 large or 2 small red onions
6 cloves of garlic, peeled
3 tablespoons olive oil
salt and cracked black pepper
18 piccolo tomatoes
18 black olives
100g feta cheese

Remove the ends from the courgettes and cut in half lengthwise. Sprinkle with salt and place face-down on paper towels. Cut the eggplant lengthwise into quarters and treat the same as the courgettes. Leave for 20–30 minutes, then wipe dry. Remove and discard the stems, seeds and white ribs from the capsicums and cut into 2cm squares. Peel the onions and cut lengthwise into eighths, leaving a tiny bit of root attached to prevent them from breaking up. Put the vegetables and garlic (but not the tomatoes) in a baking dish, brush with olive oil, season and bake in a 180°C oven for 20 minutes, or until they are cooked. Add the tomatoes for the last 5 minutes to soften slightly.

Allow the vegetables to cool, add the olives and crumble the feta cheese over the top.

To complete and serve

2–3 tablespoons olive oil
6 lamb loins
3 tablespoons wholegrain mustard

Cut the chilled Risotto Cake into rounds, triangles or squares and fry in the oil until lightly browned and heated through. Keep warm.

Trim the lamb loins of any fat or sinew, spread with mustard and roll in the Crust mixture. Seal all over in a hot frypan, transfer to a 200°C oven and bake for 5 minutes, or until cooked medium-rare. Put aside to rest for a few minutes.

Arrange the Risotto Cake on heated plates, top with the sliced lamb and arrange the Mediterranean Vegetable Salad around the edge.

Serves 6

Recommended wine:

Montana 'F' Fairhall Estate Cabernet Sauvignon

Recipe from Diane Callard

THE LANDING CAFE
LAKE TARAWERA

Top left: Mokoia Island at first light, as seen from the shore of Lake Rotorua.

Pastures and Peaks

Waikato, Central Plateau and Taranaki

New Zealand is internationally famous for its sheep, but dairy farming also plays an important part in the local economy. Drive through the Waikato city of Hamilton and on through smaller towns like picturesque Cambridge and Tirau and you will see why the country is promoted overseas as a 'clean, green land'. Verdant pasture is everywhere, and not only sheep and cows graze contentedly, but also deer, racehorses and even ostriches.

Further down the island, Lake Taupo and the busy town that sits on its shores provides some of the best trout fishing in the world. It is illegal to sell the fish, but if you catch your own most lodges, butcher's shops and the occasional restaurant will prepare it for you. A few years ago, a wily restaurateur tried to circumvent the law by listing trout on his menu as 'free' – but charging $25 for the accompanying sauce. It was an interesting concept, but he didn't get away with it.

Beyond Taupo are the spectacular volcanoes of the Central Plateau, most notably Ruapehu, Ngauruhoe and Tongariro. Skiing is a popular winter pastime for locals and visitors from around the world.

The dramatic landscape inspires the region's artists. Taupo's Penny Wilson makes the association with the land very direct, while others like sculptor Graham Cooper are content to reflect local activities.

The central location makes it easy for restaurants to source their ingredients from many parts of the country. Wine is made by a few hobbyists, but there is virtually no commercial production. That hasn't stopped enthusiasm for the product of the grape. Taupo's Scenic Cellars is one of the best retail wine outlets in the country, and restaurants like The Bach and Restaurant Villino take their wine lists very seriously indeed.

Further south, dramatic Mt Taranaki towers over New Plymouth. This carefully laid out city is not on the usual tourist beat, but it boasts a handful of excellent restaurants.

The jetty at Kuratau on the southern shores of Lake Taupo.

Seared Salmon
with artichoke and olive salad

250g salmon fillet, skinned and boned
salt and pepper to taste
1 large red onion
1 red capsicum (pepper)
4 sun-dried tomatoes
425g tin artichoke hearts
¼ cup black olives
120ml avocado oil
2 tablespoons light soy sauce
4 tablespoons mirin (Japanese cooking sake, available at Asian food stores)
juice of 1 lemon
2 tablespoons olive oil
Italian flatleaf parsley, to garnish

Cut the salmon into two pieces lengthwise, pat dry, season and put aside. Peel the onion and slice thinly. Remove and discard the stem, ribs and seeds from the capsicum and cut the flesh into thin strips. Cut the sun-dried tomatoes into strips. Drain the artichoke hearts and cut into quarters. Destone the olives if necessary. Heat 100ml of the avocado oil in a heavy frypan and fry the onion and garlic until they are soft but not brown. Add the artichokes, capsicum, sun-dried tomato, drained olives, soy sauce, mirin and lemon juice. Cook until the liquid is reduced by half, remove from the heat and cool to room temperature.

To complete and serve
Heat the olive oil in a heavy frypan and sear the salmon, cooking for 2-3 minutes each side (it should be medium-rare). Pile the salad mixture onto the serving plates and arrange the salmon on top. Drizzle with the remaining avocado oil and garnish with a sprig of Italian parsley. The dish is best served just warm.

Serves 2
Recommended wine:
Kemblefield Hawke's Bay Sauvignon Blanc

Recipe from David Kerr

THE MUSEUM CAFE
HAMILTON

Above: Doves find peace in the lush surroundings of Hamilton Gardens.

Black Forest Cheesecake

300g biscuit crumbs
3 tablespoons cocoa
2 x 420g tins cherries, pitted
1 cup caster sugar
500g cream cheese
8 leaves gelatine
500ml cream
¹/₂ cup Kirsch

Mix the biscuit crumbs and cocoa together and press into a 27cm springform tin. Drain the cherries, reserving the liquid. Cream the sugar and cream cheese together. Dissolve five of the gelatine leaves in water according to the packet directions and stir into the sugar and cream cheese. Whip the cream and fold through the mixture. Pour half into the prepared tin, and arrange the well-drained cherries on top. Pour the remaining mixture over the top to form a 'sandwich'. Refrigerate until set. Meanwhile, place the reserved cherry juice, Kirsch and the remaining gelatine leaves into a pan and heat until the gelatine is dissolved. Cool to room temperature, pour over the cheesecake and allow to set.

Serves 12
Recommended wine:
Rongopai Vintage Reserve
Riesling Selection

Recipe from Caroline Barns-Graham

THE GALLERY CAFE
CAMBRIDGE

Left: Penny Wilson's Pumice *(oil and gesso on board) is inspired by the geology and geography of the Central Plateau. It is loosely based on the idea of a cross-section or core sample. Penny, a Taupo artist, is interested in how paint can be applied in layers and wiped away in parts to reveal underlying applications, reminiscent of the strata of the volcanic Central Plateau.*

Seared Big-eye Tuna
with wilted greens, ginger and wasabi broth, sun-dried tomato polenta and shiitake mushrooms

*4 pieces big-eye tuna, approximately
180g each*

3 sprigs coriander

3 tablespoons olive oil

Pat the tuna steaks dry with paper towels. Roughly chop or tear the coriander, mix with the oil and add the tuna pieces. Stir to coat, then refrigerate overnight.

Sun-dried Tomato Polenta
30g sun-dried tomatoes
150ml cream
350ml cold water
125g polenta

Roughly chop the sun-dried tomatoes and put aside. Add the cream to the water in a large saucepan. Bring to a rapid simmer, add the polenta and stir continuously for 10 minutes (be careful – it spits as it thickens). Add the tomatoes, stirring thoroughly to make sure they are evenly distributed. Pour the mixture into a greased loaf tin lined with plastic food wrap, cover and refrigerate.

Ginger and Wasabi Broth
750ml fish stock (see Note)
¹/₂ bunch fresh coriander
4 small bok choy
1 red capsicum (pepper)
40g shiitake mushrooms, fresh if possible, or dried and soaked until soft
50g Japanese pickled ginger
1 tablespoon Kikkoman soy sauce
wasabi paste and Chinese five-spice powder to taste (both available at Asian food stores)
2 tablespoons peanut oil
2 tablespoons black sesame seeds

Bring the stock to a slow simmer. Meanwhile, chop most of the coriander, discarding the stalks but putting aside a few leaves for use as a garnish. Slice the bok choy in half lengthwise.

Remove and discard the stems, ribs and seeds from the capsicum and cut the flesh into thin strips. Thinly slice the shiitake mushrooms. Add the pickled ginger and coriander to the simmering stock and stir in the soy sauce, wasabi paste and five-spice powder to taste. Add the capsicum and mushrooms, cover and simmer until tender, and finally add the bok choy, cooking for a few more minutes. While the broth is cooking, cut the polenta into triangles or squares. Heat the peanut oil in a heavy frypan and cook the polenta pieces until lightly browned.

To complete and serve
Heat a heavy frypan until very hot, and sear the tuna briefly on all sides. It should be very rare but warm in the middle. Remove and roll in the sesame seeds, pressing to ensure a good coating, and put into the oven on a low heat to keep warm without cooking. Arrange the bok choy in heated serving bowls and place a piece of polenta on top. Slice each piece of tuna into four and arrange the pieces over the polenta. Pour the broth around the edge, ensuring that each serving gets approximately the same amount of ginger and capsicum. Garnish with the reserved coriander leaves (fennel fronds have been used in the illustration).

Note: Fish stock is now being produced commercially, but if you prefer to make your own, put fish frames and offcuts in a saucepan of cold water with a little roughly chopped onion, carrot and celery, a few peppercorns and whatever fresh herbs you have on hand. Bring to a gentle simmer, skimming the froth off the top as it forms. Cook for no more than 20 minutes, then strain through muslin.

Serves 4
Recommended wine:
Jackson Estate Pinot Noir 2000
Recipe from Alexander Obel
RESTAURANT VILLINO, TAUPO

Above: Flyfisher, *a limited edition bronze cast using the lost wax method, is by Lake Taupo sculptor Graham Cooper. Sculpture from marble and a local stone called Huka conglomerate are other favoured media of this artist, who lives and works beside the Waikato River.*

Seared Venison
with kumara frittata and port and blueberry chutney

400g venison loin
3 cloves garlic
2 sprigs thyme
2 sprigs rosemary
200ml extra virgin olive oil

Remove fat and silverskin from venison. Peel the garlic and strip the leaves from the herb sprigs. Crush together with the back of a knife, then place in a bowl with the meat. Add the oil and marinate for 4–6 hours.

Port and Blueberry Chutney

3 red onions
2 tablespoons olive oil
1kg blueberries
750ml port
150ml red wine

Peel and finely chop the onions. Heat the oil in a large saucepan and sweat the onion until it is soft but not coloured. Add the blueberries, cook for a further 2 minutes, then pour the port and wine over. Bring to the boil, flambé (light with a match or by tipping the pot towards a gas flame) and simmer for 4–6 hours, or until the fruit breaks down. Add diluted port if the mixture starts to dry out during this time. Put four tablespoons aside for use in this recipe, and store the remainder in a sealed, sterilised jar. It will last for 1–2 months, and is excellent with beef, lamb, chicken, turkey, etc.

Port Jus

1 stalk celery
1 medium carrot
2 shallots
1 tablespoon butter
200ml port
200ml veal or beef jus (reduced stock, available at good supermarkets)

Peel and dice the vegetables and sweat in the butter until softened. Add the port and flambé. When the flames have subsided, add the jus and reduce until the mixture reaches a good pouring consistency. Season and keep warm.

Kumara Frittata

1 large or 2 small golden kumara (about 200g)
3 tablespoons bourbon
1 1/2 tablespoons maple syrup
water to cover
salt to taste
butter, for greasing
1 egg
150ml cream
pepper

Wash and peel the kumara and cut into halves or thirds crosswise. Place in a saucepan with the bourbon and maple syrup, cover with cold water and season. Bring to the boil, lower the heat and simmer until just tender. Cut into 3mm-thick slices. Use the butter to grease a mini-muffin mould and divide the kumara mixture between the twelve compartments, making sure they are no more than three-quarters full. Mix the egg and cream with salt and pepper and pour over the kumara to just cover. Bake in a 200°C oven for 10–12 minutes.

To complete and serve

1 bunch spinach
2 tablespoons butter
salt and pepper

Wash the spinach well and discard the stalks. Place in a saucepan with a little salt and a splash of water. Remove the venison from the marinade and scrape off excess oil. Heat a heavy frypan very well, season the meat and sear well, turning regularly for 5–10 minutes, depending on how rare you want the meat (venison is very lean, so should be served medium-rare at most). Meanwhile, heat the reserved chutney in a small saucepan and place the frittata back in the oven to warm through. Warm the port jus. When the venison is cooked, cover loosely with foil and place in a warming drawer to rest for 5–10 minutes. Heat the spinach and cook for about a minute, until it is wilted but still bright green. Drain well. Melt the butter, toss the spinach through to coat, season then distribute among four heated serving plates. Place three frittata on top of each serving. Slice the meat crosswise into twelve slices and lean the venison slices against the frittata. Dot a little chutney on top of each slice, drizzle port jus around the edge and serve.

Serves 4
Recommended wine:
Esk Valley The Terraces

THE BACH
TAUPO

Top right: The dramatic rush of water at Huka Falls, near Taupo.

Below: Carved out of one piece of wapiti antler by Lake Taupo's Des Baker, this intricately carved Priest *administers the last rites to the 'catch of the day'. Born in Great Britain, Des attended the Doncaster School of Art and has been carving fine objects since the 1960s. He is renowned internationally for his fine netsuke work.*

Macfarlanes Eggs Benedict
with lemon hollandaise

2 hashbrowns (good commercial brand, or make your own)
1 tablespoon olive oil
1 tomato
1 tablespoon basil pesto (available at delicatessens and some supermarkets)
2 tablespoons freshly grated parmesan

Fry the hashbrowns in the olive oil until they are crisp and golden. Cut the tomato in half crosswise and dab each half with basil pesto, pile grated cheese on top and grill until melted and lightly browned. Meanwhile, make the Lemon Hollandaise (see page 189).

To complete and serve
2 eggs
2 slices smoked salmon
Lemon Hollandaise
¹/₂ avocado

Poach the eggs. Reheat the hashbrowns and grilled tomatoes and place the hashbrowns on a heated serving plate. Top each with a slice of smoked salmon, then a poached egg. Pour Lemon Hollandaise over the top and arrange the tomato halves and avocado alongside.

Serves 1
Recommended wine:
Morton Estate Sauvignon Blanc

Recipe from Tim Waite

MACFARLANES ESPRESSO BAR
NEW PLYMOUTH

Left: The dramatic volcanic cone of Mt Taranaki.

Below: Dale Copeland is a mathematician, book binder and artist. Her mixed media assemblages 'find their beauty in images of fear, death and the follies of living, using collected fragments of objects from life'. In A Different Sort of Sacrifice *Dale documents the way in which sacrifice and personal pain diminish in intensity over time.*

Above: Paul Hutchinson lives at Puniho, Okato, in Taranaki. His still life painting, landscapes and portraits are predominantly in oil. Pumpkins *(oil on board) is a still life of the artist's home-grown produce.*

Harvests and History

Hawke's Bay, Manawatu and Wanganui

*H*awke's Bay was once known as 'the fruit bowl of New Zealand', and apples, pears and other tree-borne crops still play an important role in the local economy.

But it is the product of the grape that has brought international acclaim to this long-settled region. The local soil and climate suit a wide range of wine styles, from delicate riesling to meaty syrah. Even zinfandel, normally grown on bakingly hot sites in California, shows considerable potential.

Where there is fine wine there is good food, and the Bay boasts a large number of well-regarded restaurants. Great pride is taken in local ingredients, many of which can be bought for home use from the regular farmers' markets that attract as many out-of-town visitors as locals. The markets are run under strict criteria. The people behind the stalls must be the actual producers, so they can chat knowledgeably about their wares.

Much of the local art is inspired by the landscape, but a firm link with the wine industry is made each year at a fund-raising auction for Cranford Hospice, in Hastings. Many of the bottles wear one-off labels featuring the work of local artists and craftspeople.

Architectural historians can find much to occupy them in Hawke's Bay. Napier, the region's major city, was devastated by a large earthquake in 1931 and the resultant rebuilding programme has meant that the city is now regarded as the Art Deco capital of New Zealand.

Further south lie the cities of Palmerston North and Wanganui. Both rate many mentions in textbooks covering the early battles between Maori and British soldiers, but today the grazing land around each centre is reassuringly peaceful. The region's history is often reflected in the local art, many examples of which can be seen in the nationally acclaimed Manawatu Art Gallery in Palmerston North and the Sarjeant Gallery in Wanganui.

The local soil and climate aren't suited to growing wine grapes, but restaurants and cafés take pride in offering a selection of wines from around the country.

From Te Mata Peak overlooking the Hawke's Bay landscape.

Goat Cheese Parcels
with red capsicum coulis and merlot onion marmalade

Red Capsicum Coulis
1 medium onion
1 leek
5 red capsicums (peppers)
2 cloves garlic
100g butter
1 bay leaf
1 sprig thyme
caster sugar
salt and pepper to taste
500ml tomato juice

Peel the onion, trim off and discard most of the green leaves from the leek, remove and discard the stems, ribs and seeds from the capsicums and peel the garlic. Cut all the vegetables into small dice. Melt the butter in a saucepan and add the vegetables. Cook over low heat until slightly softened, then stir in the herbs. Add sugar and seasoning to taste. Stir in the tomato juice and continue cooking until the vegetables are very soft.

Place all ingredients in a blender and process. Force the mixture through a fine sieve, adding a little water if necessary to make a thick sauce. Correct the seasoning and put aside.

Onion Marmalade
1 medium onion
1 tablespoon vegetable oil
$^{1}/_{2}$ teaspoon mustard seeds
2 tablespoons merlot or similar red wine
salt and pepper to taste

Cut the onion in half and slice very finely. Heat the oil in a heavy frypan and sweat the mustard seeds over low heat until they begin to pop. Add the sliced onion and stir. Cook until the onions begin to caramelise, then stir in the merlot. Simmer until the liquid evaporates. Season to taste.

Above: Frank Szirmay's bronze sculpture Godwit *was presented to the Hawke's Bay Airport Authority and the people of the region by the National Airways Corporation in 1977. A stylised form of the godwit, a migratory bird, was the airline's symbol.*

Above left: Napier is regarded as the Art Deco capital of New Zealand and attracts visitors from around the world to admire the many beautifully restored buildings that date back to the 1930s. Many tobacco companies avoid exterior signs that advertise their activities, but this one is of historic interest — and is part of the design detail.

Goat Cheese Parcels
4 courgettes (zucchini)
2 red or yellow capsicums (peppers)
1 clove garlic
2 tablespoons olive oil
1 x 200g packet Puhoi Golden Goat Chèvre Salade
salt and pepper to taste

Trim the ends from the courgettes. Remove and discard the stems, ribs and seeds from the capsicums. Cut three of the courgettes and both capsicums into fine strips. Peel, crush and chop the garlic clove. Heat the oil in a heavy frypan and pan-fry the vegetables with the garlic over medium heat until slightly softened (add the garlic after a few minutes to prevent it from burning). Put aside. Cut the remaining courgettes into lengthwise slices and pan-fry on one side only. Cut the goat cheese into quarters and use the courgette slices to wrap the pieces, cooked side out. Place the parcels in an ovenproof dish and place a teaspoon of Onion Marmalade on top of each. Place in a 160°C oven just to warm through.

To complete and serve
30g hazelnuts

Chop the hazelnuts and dry-fry until lightly toasted. Reheat the vegetables, place on heated serving plates and drizzle Red Capsicum Coulis around the edge. Place a warmed Goat Cheese Parcel on top of the vegetables, scatter with the hazelnuts and serve.

Serves 6–8
Recommended wine:
Kim Crawford Hawke's Bay Sauvignon Blanc

Recipe from Eddie van Druggan

ANATOLE'S RESTAURANT
THE COUNTY HOTEL
NAPIER

Pan-fried Scallops
with red capsicum cream and salad greens

Red Capsicum Cream
3 cloves garlic
1 red capsicum (pepper)
1 egg yolk
1 1/2 teaspoons grainy mustard
3 tablespoons extra virgin olive oil
3 tablespoons vegetable oil
salt and pepper to taste

Roast the garlic cloves (unpeeled) and capsicum in a 180°C oven. When the garlic cloves are soft, squeeze the flesh onto a saucer. Leave the capsicum in the oven until the skin blisters and blackens (it may be necessary to use the grill). Place in a paper bag to steam, and when cool enough to handle scrape off the skin and discard the stem, ribs and seeds. Chop the flesh until you have two or three tablespoons. Place in a food processor with two-thirds of the garlic flesh (reserve the remainder for the croutons, below), egg yolk and mustard and blend for 30 seconds. With the motor running add the oils, drop by drop, through the feed tube until the sauce reaches the consistency of mayonnaise. Season to taste and store in the refrigerator until required (may be prepared up to two days in advance).

Garlic Croutons
2 x 1cm-thick slices white bread
2 tablespoons olive or vegetable oil
salt to taste

Remove and discard the crusts from the bread and cut into 1cm cubes. Stir the garlic flesh left over from the previous recipe with the oil and salt and stir the cubes of bread through the mixture. Spread on an oven tray and roast at 180°C for a few minutes, until the croutons are golden-brown (may be prepared up to 2 hours in advance).

Chardonnay Dressing
1 tablespoon very finely chopped onion
1/2 teaspoon grainy mustard
1/2 teaspoon sugar
3 tablespoons olive or vegetable oil
3 tablespoons chardonnay (preferably Church Road)
salt and pepper to taste

Place all ingredients in a screwtop jar and shake vigorously to mix.

To finish and serve
100g salad greens or mesclun mix, torn into bite-sized pieces with hard stalks removed and discarded
24 scallops
2 tablespoons olive oil
1 clove garlic, peeled and crushed
salt and cracked black pepper to taste

Wash and thoroughly dry the salad greens and toss in the Chardonnay Dressing. Place on serving plates. Trim off and discard the hard 'boot' on the side of each scallop (usually directly opposite the roe). Heat the oil in a heavy frypan and add the scallops and garlic. Toss and cook until the scallops are just warmed through – probably around 30 seconds. Season to taste. Sprinkle the Garlic Croutons over the salad greens and place the scallops on top. Finally, drizzle Red Capsicum Cream over each serving.

Serves 4
Recommended wine:
Church Road Chardonnay

Recipe from Malcolm Redmond

CHURCH ROAD WINERY
HAWKE'S BAY

Top left: The snow-capped Tararua Range in southern Hawke's Bay overlooks land that is world renowned for the quality of its fruit and wine.

Above: Artist Nga waiata has recently returned to her Ngati Kahungunu roots. This oil on canvas, Kahurangi Nui, and her other works evoke feelings and memories associated with the sea. The constant ebb and flow of the tides is seen as a metaphor for the life-force, or mauri, the darkness and danger, the softness and elegance, perilous and gentle, the sea in all of its moods.

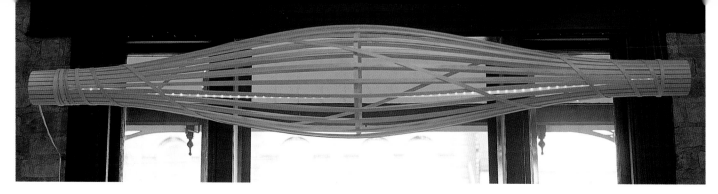

Above: This wooden lightshade by David Trubridge combines the flair of an artist with the care of a craftsman. David is one of New Zealand's best-known designers of contemporary furniture.

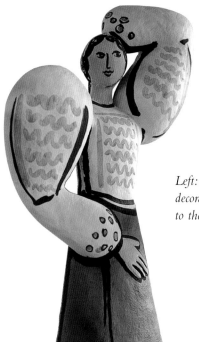

Left: Ann Verdcourt's figurine (hand-built clay decorated with stains and oxides) pays homage to the work of Henri Matisse.

Below: The rolling hills of Hawke's Bay act as a backdrop to a typical New Zealand woolshed.

Hazelnut and Raspberry Roulade

3 eggs
90g caster sugar
60g hazelnuts
1 tablespoon wholemeal flour

Separate the eggs. Beat the yolks, add the caster sugar and beat for approximately 5 minutes, or until the mixture is very pale and mousse-like (it should fall from the beaters in ribbons when they are lifted out). Meanwhile, whisk the whites until they form stiff peaks. When the mousse mixture is done, sprinkle the hazelnuts over the top and fold in, then repeat with the flour. Add half the egg whites and half-mix, half-fold in to loosen the mixture. Carefully fold in the remaining egg whites. Pour the mixture into two Swiss roll tins lined with baking paper, or use one tin with the same surface area. Level off the top and knock any egg white lumps so the mousse cooks evenly. Place in a 180°C oven for 8–10 minutes, or until the top is golden and lightly springy to touch. Leave to cool.

To complete and serve
1 tablespoon caster sugar
350g raspberries
1 teaspoon icing sugar
Vanilla Cream (see page 189)
nasturtium flowers, to garnish

Turn the roulade onto a piece of greaseproof paper and sprinkle with caster sugar. Blend 100g of the raspberries with the icing sugar until smooth. Put aside. Spread the vanilla cream over the top of the roulade and cover with raspberries. Roll carefully using the long sides, slice into portions and serve with the puréed raspberries. Garnish with the nasturtium flowers.

Serves 4
Recommended wine:
Montana Virtu
Recipe from Lesley Kingston

TAKE FIVE RESTAURANT
AND WINE BAR, NAPIER

Salmon Macaroni
served in an apple with rocket sauce

1 Gala apple
1 litre apple juice
50g rocket
1 teaspoon extra virgin olive oil
1 teaspoon rice wine vinegar
150g salmon steak
salt and pepper
3 tablespoons jasmine tea leaves
2 tablespoons organic macaroni
1 tablespoon cream

Peel and core the apple. Place the apple juice in a large saucepan, bring to the boil, add the apple and simmer until just tender. Remove with a slotted spoon and keep warm, reserving the ccoking liquid.

Meanwhile, place the rocket, oil and vinegar in a blender and process until smooth. Wipe the salmon steak and season with salt and pepper. Place the tea leaves in the bottom of a wok, heat for a few seconds then put a cake rack over the top. Place the salmon on the rack and cover the wok, using tea towels around the edge of the lid to ensure it is completely airtight. Smoke for 2 minutes.

Meanwhile, cook the macaroni according to the packet directions in the reserved apple juice. Remove when cooked, and place in a smaller saucepan with a little of the cooking liquid. Stir in the cream.

To complete and serve
Spoon the creamy macaroni into the apple, adding more cooking liquid if required. Place on a heated plate and arrange the salmon steak alongside.

Serves 1

Recommended wine:

Sileni Estates Sémillon

Recipe from Kent Baddeley

SILENI ESTATES WINERY
HASTINGS

Left: The outdoor seating area at Mesa Café overlooks the beautifully kept Sileni Estates vineyard.

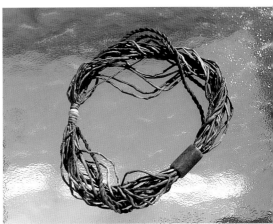

Above: Germany-born Ingrid Schloemer has used hand-dyed silk, 14-carat gold and jade for Interval. *Ingrid now lives in Hawke's Bay, and creating individual, intricate pieces of jewellery and small sculptures from gemstones and jade has become her passion. Her aim is to create organic, harmonious works that give the hands as much joy as the eye.*

Above: Peter Maclean's boxes are hand-finished and made from native New Zealand woods — these ones are kauri and paua shell. He describes them as functional, but also 'inventive, sculptural, minimal objects'. Peter works from his home by the river in Clive, where he also makes furniture.

Garlic and Thyme-rubbed Lamb Rump
on a warm vegetable salad with Kalamata olives and Parisienne potatoes

4 lamb rumps, 180–200g each
6 cloves garlic, chopped
handful lemon thyme, chopped
500ml olive oil
rock salt
cracked black pepper
1 red capsicum (pepper)
1 yellow capsicum (pepper)
¹/₂ cup olive oil
1 eggplant (aubergine)
3 courgettes (zucchini)
3 large potatoes

Trim the lamb rumps of all fat and sinew. Mix the garlic and lemon thyme with the olive oil. Add a pinch of salt and half teaspoon of black pepper, and turn the lamb rumps in the mixture, then refrigerate (this can be done up to a day in advance).

Remove and discard the stalks, ribs and seeds from the capsicums and cut into quarters. Place on an oven tray, brush with olive oil, season with rock salt and cracked pepper and roast in a 180°C oven for approximately 15 minutes, or until softened. Cut the eggplant into slices about 1cm thick and pat dry with paper towels. Season lightly. Heat three tablespoons of olive oil in a heavy frypan and cook until softened and lightly browned. Place on paper towels to dry. Trim the courgettes, cut crosswise into discs or lengthwise into 5mm slices and cook in the same frypan, adding more oil if necessary. Put aside with the eggplant.

Peel the potatoes and cut into balls, using a Parisienne baller (available at professional cooking equipment stores). Cook in boiling salted water for about 5 minutes, or until just cooked through.

Heat a little of the lamb marinade in a heavy frypan and sear the rumps on all sides. Transfer to a 180°C oven and cook for about 12 minutes, or until medium-rare. Put in a warm place to rest. Arrange four piles of capsicums, eggplant and courgettes on an oven tray and place in the oven for 3–4 minutes. Meanwhile, pan-fry the potato balls in a little oil in a frypan for the same length of time.

To complete and serve
20 kalamata olives
100ml beef jus (reduced stock)

Place a vegetable pile in the centre of each serving plate, arrange the potato balls and olives around the edge, slice the lamb and drape over the top. Drizzle the heated beef jus over the meat and garnish with any fresh herbs you have on hand.

Serves 4
Recommended wine:
Matariki Pinot Noir
Recipe from Daniel Lorch

LA POSTINA
HAVELOCK NORTH

Right: It's the Eskimo Blood in My Veins, *by Katherine Quinn (shellac and ink). Katherine has devised a method of image-making small enough to be achieved on her kitchen table. She uses paper, shellac, ink and silk tissue. Her illustration style has been influenced by the painters and architects of the early Renaissance period, with her own whimsical touches added.*

It's the eskimo blood in my veins

Right: Overlooking the Esk Valley bisected by the Napier-Taupo highway, which links Hawke's Bay to the Central Plateau. The region was once known as the 'fruit bowl of New Zealand'. Now it is the local wine that is catching the world's imagination — although fruit still plays an important role in the local economy.

Right: This landscape (oil pastel on paper), reminiscent of the rolling hills of Southern Hawke's Bay, is by young Auckland artist Hannah Sheahan.

Mussel Cakes
with lime and poppy seed dressing and avocado

2kg mussels
¹/₂ cup dry white wine
1 large red onion
3 spring onions
2 cups flour
¹/₂ teaspoon salt
2 tablespoons sweet chilli sauce (any brand)
3 tablespoons chopped coriander
2 teaspoons lemon juice
4 eggs

Scrub, rinse and pull the beards from the mussels, then place in a wok or large saucepan with the wine and half a cup of water. Bring to the boil, covered, and leave the lid in place for approximately 20 seconds. Remove the mussels as their shells open. Remove the flesh and chop roughly. Chop the red onion into fine dice. Trim the spring onions and slice thinly. Mix all the ingredients together to form a thick batter.

To complete and serve
vegetable oil for pan-frying
2 avocados, peeled and destoned
lemon juice (to prevent browning)
salt and pepper to taste
salad greens
Lime and Poppy Seed Dressing (see page 189)

Heat a little oil in a heavy frypan and spoon in the mussel batter, two tablespoons at a time. When the fritters begin to set, place in a 180°C oven. Turn over once when nearly cooked. Meanwhile, mash the avocado with the lemon juice. Season to taste and put aside. When the fritters are cooked place on heated serving plates, top with a spoonful of avocado, surround with salad greens and drizzle the dressing over the top.

Serves 4–5

Recommended wine:

Vidal Estate Chardonnay

Recipe from Kylie Howard

VIDAL WINE BAR, HASTINGS

Above: Born in Cape Town, South Africa, Des Robertshaw emigrated to New Zealand in 1961. Largely self-taught, he works in acrylic paint using bold, strong colours and linear design, as in Aqua *(acrylic on board). Des's paintings capture New Zealand's unique purity of light and the essence of the land and the people of the Hawke's Bay.*

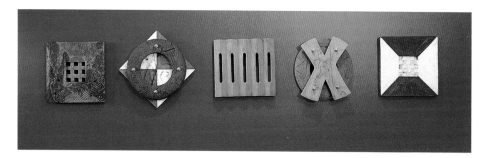

Above: Ceramic artist Linda Bruce uses clay, found objects and metals to create unique artworks such as this set of five pieces entitled Medium Components. *Linda's work involves the relationship between shape and form, texture and colour. Using techniques of bolting, binding and piercing Linda creates plays of shape and form, texture, colour and pattern. She draws her inspiration from history, modern life and the landscape of rural Hawke's Bay, and her work ranges from the light-hearted to the serious.*

Cervena on Carbonara Risotto
with tomato and chilli relish

Tomato and Chilli Relish
500g tomatoes
1 red onion
1 small red chilli
1 clove garlic
1 tablespoon brown sugar
100ml balsamic vinegar
salt and pepper

Cut a cross into the stem end of the tomatoes, place in boiling water for 20 seconds and refresh in cold water. Peel and deseed, then roughly chop the flesh. Peel and roughly chop the red onion. Remove and discard the seeds from the chilli and chop. Peel and chop the garlic. Place the chopped ingredients and sugar in a blender or food processor and process briefly, leaving the mixture a little chunky. Place in a saucepan with the balsamic vinegar and gently simmer over low heat for 2 hours. Season to taste. This can be made a day in advance.

Carbonara Risotto
1 litre chicken stock, preferably home-made
250g bacon rashers
3 cloves garlic
small bunch Italian flatleaf parsley
1 tablespoon olive oil
400g arborio rice
100g freshly grated parmesan
200ml cream
salt and pepper to taste

Bring the stock to the boil and keep at a gentle simmer. Remove the rinds from the bacon and chop the rashers into fine dice. Peel the garlic and chop finely. Chop the parsley leaves. Heat the olive oil and cook the chopped bacon for 2–3 minutes. Remove and put aside. Add the garlic to the pot, stir briefly, then add the rice. Stir until it becomes translucent then add 200ml stock. Turn down the heat and keep adding stock, bit by bit, until the rice is cooked but still retains a little al dente bite (about 20–25 minutes). Remove from the heat and stir in the bacon, parsley, parmesan and cream. Season, cover and allow to stand for 3–4 minutes.

To complete and serve
6 x 180–200g Cervena Denver leg steaks
salt and pepper
2 tablespoons olive oil
36 asparagus spears

Trim the Cervena steaks if necessary and season. Heat the olive oil in a heavy frypan and sear on both sides. Transfer to a 180°C oven for 6–8 minutes (they should be rare). Rest for 3–4 minutes. Meanwhile, peel the asparagus spears from a point 1cm below the start of the flower head and snap off the tough bases (this step is optional, depending on freshness). Trim and cook in boiling salted water until just tender.

To serve, spoon the risotto onto heated plates and place the asparagus spears on top. Slice the Cervena and drape the asparagus over. Spoon a little relish over each serving.

Serves 6
Recommended wine:
Clearview Estate Cape
Kidnappers Merlot

Recipe from Shane Flanagan

DEJEUNER RESTAURANT
PALMERSTON NORTH

Marinated Chicken Breast
on Hokkien noodles with shiitake and bok choy stir-fry

4 boneless chicken breasts, skin on
4 tablespoons light soy sauce
2 tablespoons sesame oil
1 teaspoon fish sauce
4 tablespoons maple syrup
1 clove garlic, peeled and chopped
1 teaspoon chopped ginger
generous pinch cracked black pepper

Trim any excess fat from the chicken breasts. Mix all other ingredients in a bowl and use to marinate the chicken overnight.

Noodle Sauce
2 tablespoons light soy sauce
1 tablespoon sesame oil
¹/₂ teaspoon fish sauce
2 tablespoons maple syrup
¹/₂ teaspoon chopped ginger
¹/₂ clove garlic, peeled and chopped
1 tablespoon sweet chilli sauce
2 teaspoons sesame seeds
200ml water

Mix all ingredients together and put aside until required.

To complete and serve
60g shiitake mushrooms
2 small bunches bok choy
1 tablespoon butter
400g Hokkien noodles

Remove and discard the hard ends from the mushroom stalks and slice the caps. Cut the ends from the bok choy bunches, allowing the leaves to separate.

Remove the chicken from the marinade and lightly brown in a hot pan. Transfer to a 200°C oven until cooked (about 20 minutes, depending on size). Meanwhile, melt the butter in a wok or large frypan and add the mushrooms and bok choy leaves. Fry, stirring, for 3 minutes, then add the noodles and Noodle Sauce. Heat through and allow the sauce to reduce and the noodles to cook (about 3 minutes).

To serve, divide the noodle mixture among four heated plates, slice each chicken breast into three diagonally and arrange on top. At Legends, the dish is garnished with strips of red capsicum, snow pea shoots and coriander.

Serves 4
Recommended wine:
Longridge Hawke's Bay
Gewürztraminer

Recipe from Hayden Robinson
LEGENDS CAFE/RESTAURANT
WANGANUI

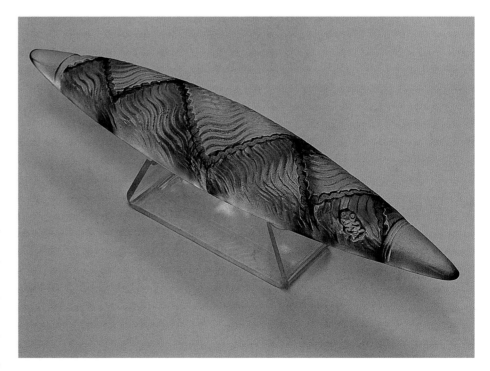

Above: This view shows the patterned underside of a unique cast crystal glass waka, one of a series of glass waka created by Wanganui artist Greg Hall. Greg's work has earned him national recognition as one of the country's leading glass artists.

Merlot-marinated Lamb Fillets
with rosemary potatoes and mint salsa

8 lamb fillets
2 cloves garlic
¹/₂ glass merlot (any good brand)

Trim all fat and sinew from the lamb. Peel and crush the garlic and add to the lamb with the wine. Marinate for at least 2 hours.

Rosemary Potatoes
10 small 'gourmet' potatoes
1 clove garlic
2 sprigs rosemary
¹/₂ cup olive oil

Scrub the potatoes, peel and crush the garlic and strip the leaves from the rosemary. Place all in a roasting dish, toss and bake in a 200°C oven for 20–30 minutes.

To complete and serve
Mint Salsa (see page 189)

Remove the lamb from the marinade, scrape off excess oil and grill or pan-fry for 2–4 minutes, turning to brown all over. Distribute the potatoes between two heated serving plates, slice each lamb fillet into three and arrange over the potatoes. Check the salsa for seasoning and spoon a 'line' over each serving. A simple green salad makes a good accompaniment.

Serves 2
Recommended wine:
Babich Pinot Noir

AMADEUS RIVERBANK CAFE
WANGANUI

Above: An iconic New Zealand cabbage tree frames this view of Rotokawau (Virginia Lake) in Wanganui. The cabbage tree, ti kouka, was an important resource for Maori, providing food, clothing and decorative items.

Capital Culture

Wairarapa and Wellington

*A*s capital city and home to Parliament, Wellington is New Zealand's seat of power. That gives it an air of confidence that is reflected in its hundreds of cafés and restaurants – Wellingtonians love to dine out.

Art plays a major part in the local social scene. Not only does the city boast a huge number of galleries, but theatre in its many forms thrives. Operas and plays regularly sell out within hours, and other cultural events are invariably crowded. The month-long International Festival of the Arts attracts artists and performers from all over the world and is the envy of the country's other major centres.

Wellington's many restaurateurs promote wines from around the country with knowledge and enthusiasm, but they take particular pride in the products of nearby Wairarapa.

Despite being one of the country's newest wine regions, the area that radiates out from the village of Martinborough has built a reputation that extends all over the world. It has hung its future on the notoriously fickle pinot noir grape, but many other varieties thrive in the local conditions. Sauvignon blanc, chardonnay, riesling, gewürztraminer and even heat-loving syrah are among the styles for which the region is nationally and internationally renowned.

Food served in the local cafés and restaurants is designed to be wine-friendly. The Wairarapa has long been a popular holiday destination for weekend refugees from the city, but nowadays they can expect to dine out as well as they can back home. Accommodation, whether it is at a vineyard or in a historic building, is also of a high standard.

The annual Toast Martinborough festival partners local wineries with top entertainers and chefs, providing an unrivalled wine and food experience. Tickets are restricted to ensure that the food and wine on offer can be sampled in relative comfort, which means thousands of enthusiasts from around the country are disappointed each year.

A trip to Wellington and the nearby Wairarapa is a rewarding experience for anybody interested in fine wine and food.

Castlepoint Lighthouse on the wild Wairarapa coast, east of Masterton.

Jewelled Corned Beef
with horseradish mash

1 red capsicum (pepper) or 1 jar roasted red pepper strips
1kg corned beef silverside
10 pimiento-stuffed green olives
6 gherkins
1 tablespoon golden syrup
$^1/_4$ cup white wine vinegar
1 bay leaf
6 black peppercorns

If using a fresh capsicum, roast or grill in a hot oven until the skin blisters and blackens. Place in a brown paper bag to steam, then scrape off the skin. Remove and discard the stem, ribs and seeds. Cut into 1cm strips. Use a small-bladed knife or sharpening tool to make tunnels in the beef. Stuff the holes with capsicum strips, olives and gherkins in any order you please. Place the beef in a heavy saucepan and cover with cold water. Add the remaining ingredients, bring to the boil and simmer for 1 hour. Remove from the heat and leave in the liquid to cool.

Horseradish Mash
8 floury potatoes
2 tablespoons fresh grated horseradish
$^1/_2$ cup cream
salt and pepper to taste

Peel the potatoes, place in a large saucepan of salted water and boil until soft. Drain and shake the pan over the element to dry completely. Mash the potatoes, add the horseradish, warm the cream and stir into the mixture. Season to taste. Drain the beef and serve sliced, with Horseradish Mash and your choice of seasonal vegetables.

Serves 6–8
Recommended wine:
Borthwick Estate
Cabernet/Merlot/Malbec

Recipe from Nicky and Darkie Brindle
TOADS LANDING, MASTERTON

Left: Wildflowers at Toads Landing.

Left: If I Sit Here Long Enough I'll See the Stars *(acrylic on canvas) is by mixed media artist Sally Reweti-Gould, who is based in Wellington. The use of bold colour with layering and added text is typical of her work. Finding positivity and beauty in the ordinary and commonplace is a favourite theme in her work.*

Left: Kura Puke is an artist of Te Atiawa descent, and her Maori ancestry is the primary focus of her work. This work, Beneath the Surface (oil on board), is concerned with the many layers that make up the land, and the historical, genealogical and spiritual layers that give added meaning to the land.

Below: Working from his Wellington studio Nick Dryden has exhibited extensively and produced many commissioned works that are held in private collections and overseas. His sculptures are created in a variety of media including marble, bronze and copper. Shag on Pole (copper and totara) is one of a series of pukeko and shags that captures the many endearing expressions and movements of these birds.

Roast Chicken
with marinated tomatoes and yoghurt garlic sauce

1 red onion, thinly sliced
4 boneless chicken breasts, skin on
2 lemons, unpeeled, 1 thinly sliced
3 sprigs oregano, chopped
5 tablespoons olive oil
sea salt and freshly ground black pepper
4 ripe tomatoes
3 sprigs Italian flatleaf parsley
1 tablespoon red wine vinegar
2 cloves garlic
1 cup plain unsweetened yoghurt

Spread the onion over the bottom of a baking dish and place the chicken breasts, skin-side up, on top. Arrange the lemon slices over the chicken. Sprinkle with oregano, two tablespoons of olive oil and seasoning. Refrigerate for 4 hours.

Slice the tomatoes. Chop the parsley and sprinkle over the top, along with a little sea salt. Drizzle with a tablespoon of olive oil and the red wine vinegar, toss carefully and leave to steep for an hour.

Peel the garlic and crush with a quarter teaspoon of sea salt. Mix with the yoghurt and leave for an hour.

To complete and serve
20 asparagus spears or seasonal green vegetable

Remove the chicken from the marinade and pat dry. Heat remaining olive oil in a heavy pan and fry the chicken, skin-side down, until golden. Return to the baking dish, skin-side up, drizzle with olive oil and the juice of the remaining lemon and cook in a 180°C oven for 10 minutes, or until cooked. Meanwhile, trim and boil the asparagus in salted water until just cooked. Serve the chicken with yoghurt sauce over the top and the drained tomato salad and asparagus alongside.

Serves 4
Recommended wine:
Gladstone Wairarapa Chardonnay

Recipe from James Reddington
CAFE CECILLE, MASTERTON

Breast and Confit of Duck
with Jerusalem artichoke tarts and puy lentil jus

6 duck breasts
1 teaspoon Maldon sea salt
$^1/_2$ teaspoon freshly ground black pepper
zest of 1 orange

Trim the duck breasts. Remove any obvious excess fat, but don't discard it – it will be used for the confit. Score the skin in a criss-cross pattern, sprinkle with salt, pepper and orange zest and refrigerate.

Duck Leg Confit
6 duck legs
1 small sprig fresh rosemary
2 teaspoons Maldon sea salt
$^1/_2$ teaspoon freshly ground black pepper
1 teaspoon Chinese five-spice powder
(available at Asian food stores)
zest of 3 oranges
500g block lard

Trim excess fat from the legs and remove the thighbones. Reserve. Use a very sharp knife to remove the top joint from the remaining bone and cut away the tendons. Carefully scrape the bone clean (this step is optional, but makes the finished dish look more attractive). Strip the leaves from the rosemary sprig and chop finely. Sprinkle the legs with the salt, pepper, five-spice powder, orange zest and rosemary. Cover and refrigerate overnight.

The next day, place all the trimmings from the breasts and legs in an oven dish and arrange the marinated legs on top. Melt the lard and pour over the legs, making sure they are completely covered. Cover the surface with baking paper and bake in a 160°C oven for 2$^1/_2$ hours. Remove from the oven and allow to cool for an hour before straining off the fat and the stock liquid that will have formed. Refrigerate long enough to set the fat, making it easier to separate from the stock which will form the basis for the sauce.

Jerusalem Artichoke Tarts
500g Jerusalem artichokes, peeled and cut up
1 cup milk
2 cups water
1 teaspoon salt
½ cup cream
½ teaspoon grated nutmeg
1½ tablespoons butter
salt and pepper
6 precooked blind-baked short crust pastry cases
2 tablespoons freshly shaved parmesan

Simmer the artichokes in the milk, water and salt for approximately 15 minutes, or until soft. Meanwhile, heat the cream with the nutmeg until reduced by half. Place the cooked artichoke pieces in a food processor and blend with the cream and butter until smooth. Season to taste. Spoon into the pastry cases and sprinkle with the shaved parmesan. Put aside.

To complete and serve
Puy Lentil Jus (see page 189)
1½ tablespoons unsalted butter
sprigs fresh oregano and thyme, to garnish

Heat two medium-sized heavy frypans and add a little confit fat to each. Pan-fry the legs, skin-side down, for 5 minutes. At the same time, pan-fry the breasts in the other frypan, skin-side down, for 10 minutes, or until golden. Turn over and season lightly. Put the legs, the reserved Jerusalem Tarts and the breasts in a 200°C oven. Remove the breasts after 5 minutes and put aside in a warm place to rest. Bake the legs and tarts for a further 10 minutes.

Just before serving, bring the reserved stock back to low heat and combine with the lentils. Stir in the butter, bit by bit, until a good sauce consistency is reached. Pile onto heated plates and arrange the breasts and legs on top. Place the tarts alongside and garnish with the fresh herbs.

Serves 6
Recommended wine:
Walnut Ridge Martinborough Pinot Noir

Recipe from Gerald Brown
and Glenys Almao
WAKELIN HOUSE, GREYTOWN

Above: A whimsical cast-steel sculpture of a group of musicians by art tutor Graeme Foster ornaments a Martinborough garden.

Right: From a series of bronze sculptures based on relationships, Push Me Pull You *has been cast from polystyrene and sand by Wellington artist Nick Dryden. Each mould can be used only once, so each sculpture is unique.*

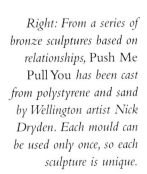

Eggplant and Goat Cheese Parcels
with dukkah, dates and mint

1 medium eggplant (aubergine)
1 teaspoon salt
5 tablespoons olive oil
freshly ground black pepper
200g fresh goat cheese
4 mandarins
¹/₂ avocado
4 fresh dates
4 sprigs mint
3–4 tablespoons cold-pressed avocado oil
4 level teaspoons dukkah (available at good food stores)

Cut the eggplant lengthwise into eight slices. Sprinkle with salt, leave for 10 minutes then rinse and pat dry. Heat the olive oil in a non-stick frypan and gently fry the slices until they are golden and silky. Season with pepper, adding more salt only if necessary. Divide the cheese into eight pieces and wrap each cube in two eggplant slices to make neat parcels. Refrigerate until needed.

To complete and serve
Segment the mandarins, scoop the flesh from the avocado and dice, split the dates and remove the stones. Finely chop the mint leaves. Place the eggplant parcels in a 160°C oven just to warm through (the cheese should be soft, but not melted). Place on heated plates and top with the mandarins, dates, mint and avocado. Drizzle with avocado oil and sprinkle with dukkah before serving.

Serves 4
Recommended wine:
Martinborough Vineyard
Pinot Gris

Recipe from Mark Limacher

ROXBURGH BISTRO
WELLINGTON

Above: Apartment blocks rise from the shore of Oriental Bay, a popular spot for Wellingtonians who like to jog, cycle, roller-blade or simply stroll around the pleasant waterfront.

Left: Descended from Ngati Porou, internationally acclaimed artist Robyn Kahukiwa is currently living in Wellington. Her works are instinctive rather than academic. They have a narrative folk style that includes elements and motifs from traditional Maori art and legend, focusing on mana Maori and mana wahine. This work is from a series called 'Nga Tuahine', which means 'sisters', and it is painted with acrylic and watercolour on hand-made Indian cotton paper.

Left: Richard's Angelic Cup and Saucer *celebrates the culture of drinking tea. It is mid-fire porcelain with a copper and tin glaze.*
Right: Wellington ceramic artist Richard Stratton's A Thinking Man's Thinking Man *refers to the nature of the father/son relationship. It is of slab construction and figurative modelling with slips and underglazes.*

Left: In Pacific Gateway *(oil on canvas), one of a series of five paintings by Wellington artist Sarah Beesley, the whare frames the landscape beyond giving a spiritual nurturing quality.*

Tangelo Crème Caramel

Caramel
115g caster sugar
5 tablespoons water

Combine sugar and water in a small saucepan. Cook over high heat without stirring until deep amber in colour. Divide between ten small moulds, coating the base.

Custard
about 4 tangelos (zest from 2, and enough extra tangelos to make 225ml juice)
700ml cream
150g caster sugar
3 whole eggs
9 egg yolks

Pour the tangelo juice through a strainer into a pot, bring to the boil and reduce by half. Cool slightly. Scald the cream with the sugar and zest over very low heat. Whisk the whole eggs and yolks together and slowly add the scalded cream, continuing to whisk gently, and finally add the reduced tangelo juice. Skim the surface of any foam. Strain through a fine sieve into a jug and use to fill the moulds, leaving a gap of about 2mm at the top. Pierce any bubbles with the point of a knife. Place in a water bath, cover and cook in a 125°C oven until just set (about 35 minutes). Chill for at least 4 hours before turning out. In the photograph, the crème carmel is served with poached Central Otago apricots and candied orange zest.

Serves 10
Recommended wine:
Palliser Noble Riesling

Recipe from Alister Brown
Logan-Brown, Wellington

Far left: Houses hug the hillsides of Wellington. Steep steps and cable-drawn chairs are a way of life for some residents of the nation's capital city.

Lamb with Black Pudding Polenta

1 litre milk
250g coarse polenta
100g black pudding, skinned and dried
salt and pepper
4 lamb short-loin pieces
1 tablespoon dried porcini powder (available at good delicatessens)
2 tablespoons olive oil

Bring the milk to the boil in a large pot, stir in the polenta and cook over low heat for 15 minutes, stirring from time to time (watch out for spitting). Stir the black pudding into the polenta. Season to taste. Spread 2cm thick on a tray and refrigerate. When cool, cut into any shapes you fancy, place on a greased tray and reheat in a 180°C oven.

Trim the lamb, rub with porcini powder and season. Heat the olive oil in a heavy frypan and cook for 1 minute on each side. Transfer to a 200°C oven and continue to cook for 2 minutes more, or longer if you prefer your meat less rare.

To complete and serve
16–20 flat mushrooms, trimmed and wiped
salt and pepper
3 tablespoons olive oil
4 tablespoons jus (reduced stock or gravy)

Slice the mushroom caps into ¹/₂cm pieces and season. Heat the oil in the same pan and cook the mushrooms until they are lightly browned. Meanwhile, heat the jus in the pan in which the lamb was cooked, stirring in the brown bits. To serve, slice the lamb and place on heated plates with the polenta and mushrooms alongside. Drizzle with the jus.

Serves 4
Recommended wine:
Martinborough Vineyard Pinot Noir

Recipe from Rex Morgan

BOUQUET GARNI, WELLINGTON
Far right: A calm day at the Port Nicholson Yacht Club.

Haven of Creativity

Nelson and Marlborough

*T*he short ferry trip from Wellington to Picton is one of the most spectacular in the country, if not the world.

The placid Marlborough Sounds with their edging of steep, bush-clad hills provide a peerless scenic introduction to the South Island. As a bonus, the stillness of the water can be a relief after crossing often-rough Cook Strait.

Until the 1980s, few people in other parts of the world had heard of Marlborough. That changed when visionary Frank Yukich, then head of Montana wines, produced the first wine from vines he had planted in the early 1970s. Sauvignon blanc was the variety that made the world's wine lovers sit up and take notice. Grown on the pebble-strewn river flats of the Wairau Valley, its grapes have an unrivalled intensity of flavour. Now, Marlborough is the largest wine-growing area in the country, and its sauvignon blanc is hailed overseas as the first truly new wine style of the past 100 years.

It is not the only variety to do well. Chardonnay, riesling, pinot gris, gewürztraminer and – more recently – pinot noir have shown an affinity for the local soil and climate, and the region is also home to most of the country's sparkling wines.

Marlborough wine is fresh and instantly appealing, and the same can be said for much of its food. Green-lipped mussels and salmon are farmed extensively in the Sounds and are featured on nearly every local restaurant menu.

Wine is important, too, across the rugged hills of Nelson, but it doesn't play as vital a role in the local economy. Rather, this picturesque region is known as a haven for artists and artisans. Glassblowers, potters, silversmiths, sculptors, painters, weavers, ceramicists and woodcarvers work in a wide range of styles, and their creations can be seen in galleries and private collections throughout New Zealand and overseas.

Some tourists miss the top of the South Island by travelling direct from Wellington to Christchurch. That's a shame. This fascinating region offers some of the best experiences in the country.

Developing vineyards in the Awatere Valley.

Fillet of Baby Salmon
with freshwater crayfish

4 baby salmon fillets, skin on, plus the fish heads and frames
1 shallot
1 small onion
130ml olive oil
1 bouquet garni (parsley stalk, celery stick, thyme and bay leaf tied into a bundle)
salt and freshly ground pepper
1 large sprig basil
1 tablespoon butter
1 tomato
1 small fennel bulb
juice of ¹/₂ lemon
8 live freshwater crayfish (koura)
fresh dill and parsley

When you purchase the salmon fillets, ask your fishmonger to give you the heads and frames. Peel and finely chop the shallot and onion. Heat two tablespoons of the oil in a saucepan and sweat the shallot and onion until soft but not brown. Chop the salmon bones and add to the pan, along with the heads and bouquet garni. Cover with cold water, add a small pinch of salt and pepper and bring to the boil. Turn down the heat and simmer gently for approximately 5 minutes, then strain through a fine sieve.

Place the stock back in the pot and boil to reduce to about four tablespoons. Crumble three-quarters of the basil leaves in your hands and add, cover for a further 5 minutes and strain. Chop the remaining basil.

Return the stock to the heat and whisk in the remaining olive oil, adding it in a thin stream. Stir in the butter and season to taste. You should now have a smooth, creamy sauce.

Cut a shallow cross in the stem end of each tomato and plunge into boiling water for 20 seconds, then into cold water. Peel, deseed, and chop the flesh. Remove and discard the root from the fennel bulb, trim and slice thinly. Blanch in boiling salted water and refresh. Stir the vegetables into the sauce, along with

the lemon juice and chopped basil. Keep warm but not hot, or it will separate.

Brush the salmon fillets with olive oil and sear in a very hot pan, turning once. They should be cooked to medium-rare after about a minute. Meanwhile, plunge the crayfish into a large pot of boiling, salted water and cook for 1 minute (they will die instantly). Keep warm.

To complete and serve
Divide the sauce among four heated serving plates. Place a salmon fillet on top and garnish with the crayfish, fresh dill and parsley.

Serves 4
Recommended wine:
Huia Gewürztraminer

Recipe from Lothar and Tracy Greiner

MARLBOROUGH TERRANEAN
PICTON

Right: The ferry trip from Wellington to Picton is one of the most scenic in the world.

Right: Paul de Jager has lived in Golden Bay for 20 years. He draws on his Ngati Awa ancestry as an inspiration for much of his work. Known for his sculptural forms and burnished bowls using locally sourced ochre, Paul has included in his recent work a series of kaitiaki or guardian heads. These works are a fusion of the Buddhist ideas of tranquillity and meditation with the Maori tradition of protecting gardens with a magic talisman.

Grilled Tarakihi in a Pasta Mille-feuille
with sautéed fennel and Champagne sauce

Pasta
100g high-grade white flour
1 egg
1 tablespoon olive oil

Place the flour in a bowl, form a well in the centre and break the egg into it. Work the flour into the egg, add the oil and knead into a smooth, medium-firm dough. Cover with plastic food wrap and refrigerate for 2 hours. When well chilled, turn onto a lightly floured surface and roll out to a 1mm-thick sheet (or use a pasta machine). Use a pastry cutter to cut out twelve 7cm-diameter circles. Bring a large amount of water to the boil, salt generously and cook the pasta circles for 2 minutes. Plunge immediately into cold water and strain.

Sautéed Fennel
2 large fennel bulbs
1 tablespoon olive oil
1 tablespoon butter
100ml dry white wine
salt and pepper to taste
juice of $^{1}/_{2}$ lemon
3–4 chervil sprigs, roughly chopped

Halve the fennel bulbs lengthwise and remove the root and any tough tops. Cut into thin slices. Heat the oil and butter in a medium-sized saucepan and sauté the fennel until it is golden and glossy. Add the wine and continue to cook over low heat for 2 minutes. Season with salt, pepper and lemon juice and sprinkle with the chervil.

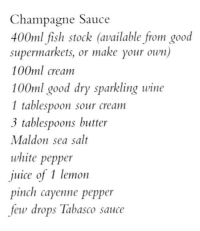

Champagne Sauce
400ml fish stock (available from good
supermarkets, or make your own)
100ml cream
100ml good dry sparkling wine
1 tablespoon sour cream
3 tablespoons butter
Maldon sea salt
white pepper
juice of 1 lemon
pinch cayenne pepper
few drops Tabasco sauce

Put stock, cream and sparkling wine in a saucepan and boil until reduced by one-third. Stir in the sour cream and butter, then season with the salt, pepper, lemon juice, cayenne pepper and Tabasco sauce. Use a balloon whisk or hand-held beater to whisk the sauce until it goes frothy.

To complete and serve
8 x 60g pieces tarakihi, boned but with
skin left on
Maldon sea salt
pepper
juice of 1 lemon
2 tablespoons each olive oil and butter

Wipe the fish with paper towels and season with salt, pepper and lemon juice. Heat the olive oil in a heavy frypan and sear the fish, skin side down, for about 2 minutes, or until the skin is golden-brown and crisp. Turn and sear the other side for 10 seconds. Remove from the pan and keep warm.

Melt the butter in a frypan. Dip the pasta circles into boiling water for 5 seconds, then coat with the butter. Warm the Sautéed Fennel and put a spoonful in the centre of each heated serving plate. Alternate the pasta circles, fennel and tarakihi until all the ingredients are used up. Drizzle with the Champagne Sauce.

Serves 4
Recommended wine:
Herzog Pinot Gris

Recipe from Louis Schindler

HERZOG RESTAURANT
BLENHEIM

Above: Originally from Holland, Lydia Geldolf now lives in Rarangi. Her limestone sculpture Dancing the Rhythms *reflects her love of the human form and its singularity.*

Roast Salmon
on Colcannon
in a bean and tomato ragout

1 whole 1–1.5kg salmon, filleted, scaled and boned, or 4 salmon steaks
150g green beans
1 clove garlic
1 tablespoon olive oil
²/₃ cup tomato juice

If using salmon fillets, place on top of one another with the skin facing outward and the tail ends opposite one another. Roll tightly in plastic food wrap and tie both ends to form a tight cylinder. Allow to firm up for at least 3–4 hours in the refrigerator. When firm, cut into 200g portions, still in the wrapping, then remove plastic and tie with cotton string.

To make the ragout, top and tail the beans and cook in salted boiling water for 1–2 minutes. Drain and cut into 2cm lengths. Peel and finely chop the garlic and sweat in the olive oil, but don't let it colour. Add the tomato juice and bring to the boil. Add the beans and simmer for 5 minutes. Season and keep warm.

To complete and serve
Colcannon (see page 189)
2 tablespoons olive oil
salt and pepper

Brush the salmon with oil, season and sear on a hot grill pan, turning to achieve a crosshatched pattern. Place in a 200°C oven for 5–8 minutes, or until just cooked. Place a pile of Colcannon in the centre of each heated serving plate, remove the string from the salmon, if used, and arrange on top. Drizzle three tablespoons of ragout around the edge and garnish with fresh thyme.

Serves 4
Recommended wine:
Daniel Le Brun Méthode
Champenoise Brut

Recipe from Niall O'Meara

CELLIER LE BRUN
RESTAURANT, MARLBOROUGH

Above: The fusion of Jack Honeywell's woodwork and Pamela Byrne's shades creates a three-dimensional functioning light art form. Lotus Lamp (top) is an up-light based on a floral design and possesses a regal tone. The stand is oak and the shade is recycled copper wire lined with hand-made harakeke paper and covered with papier mâché. Light Siesta, inspired by a sombrero and Mexican designs, is made from willow and elm. The shade is recycled copper wire lined with hand-made paper and finished in tapa cloth.

Soy-marinated Rare Beef

with gingered coriander rice cake, mesclun salad and mirin dressing

2cm piece ginger
2–3 mild red chillies
1 clove garlic
120ml Kikkoman soy sauce
100ml sesame oil
2 tablespoons caster sugar
170ml rice wine vinegar
4 tablespoons mirin (Japanese cooking sake)
660g piece beef eye fillet
2 tablespoons olive oil
salt and pepper

Peel and finely chop the ginger, deseed and chop the chillies, and peel and finely chop the garlic. Whisk with all other ingredients, place in a deep container and refrigerate until required.

Trim the fillet, removing all fat, skin and membrane. Brush with the olive oil, season and sear all over on a very hot griddle plate or barbecue. Cover loosely and put aside for about 15 minutes. When cool, prick all over with a skewer and immerse in the marinade, turning to ensure good coverage. Leave it for 4–5 hours (it can be marinated for up to 3 days, but the vinegar will 'cook' it, changing the texture).

Rice Cakes
1cm piece ginger
1–2 mild red chillies
1 bunch coriander
5 tablespoons rice wine vinegar
50g palm sugar (1 cake) or 3 tablespoons caster sugar
200g sushi rice, or short grain rice
1 tablespoon vegetable oil
2 tablespoons desiccated coconut

Peel and finely chop the ginger, deseed and chop the chillies, chop the coriander leaves (you should have approximately half a cup). Simmer the ginger with the vinegar and sugar until a syrup forms.

Remove from the heat and reserve. Thoroughly wash the rice and drain. Place in a pot and fill with cold water to a level approximately one thumbnail above the rice. Cover and bring to a gentle heat. Cook for approximately 8 minutes, by which time the rice should be glossy, plump and slightly sticky, but not crunchy. Brush a 20cm square platter or tray with the oil and spread the rice out 1.5cm thick. Leave to cool slightly.

When cool, drizzle the vinegar and ginger mixture over the rice, mixing in a little at a time until it turns silky and slightly tacky. Add the chopped chillies, coconut and coriander and stir to mix. Cover with plastic food wrap and press back to the original shape (another tray on top will make this easier). Refrigerate until firm, then cut into one or two triangles per serving.

To complete and serve
2 tablespoons canola oil
salt and pepper
mesclun salad
2 tablespoons toasted sesame seeds

Lift the beef from the marinade and cut into thin slices. Line four cups with the slices and continue adding the slices until the cups are full. Whisk the beef marinade to combine the flavours and pour half a cup into a blender or food processor. Drizzle in the canola oil and process until the dressing goes slightly thick. Season to taste.

Tip the beef 'moulds' carefully onto the serving plates. Place a Rice Cake on its edge alongside, and arrange a little mesclun salad on the other side. Drizzle everything with the dressing and sprinkle the sesame seeds over the top.

Serves 4
Recommended wine:
Domaine Georges Michel Vintage Lane Pinot Noir

Recipe from Simon Kelly

LA VERANDAH RESTAURANT
MARLBOROUGH

Steamed Mussels and Cockles
in green curry sauce

110g jar John West green curry paste
4 x 400ml tins coconut cream
^{1}/$_3$ cup Thai fish sauce (available at Asian food stores)
^{1}/$_2$ cup pineapple juice
90g brown sugar
zest and juice of 1 lemon
3 fresh kaffir lime leaves, thinly sliced

Place all ingredients in a large pot, bring to the boil and simmer for 5 minutes. This recipe makes more than you need – the extra can be kept in the refrigerator for up to a week.

1kg mussels
1kg cockles
2 tablespoons vegetable oil

Scrub the mussels and pull out the beards. Scrub the cockles and place them in a large bowl of lightly salted water for 30 minutes to disgorge any sand. Heat the oil in a wok or large pan, add the shellfish then pour over a cup of the sauce. Cover and simmer for 3–4 minutes, shaking from time to time, until all the shellfish have opened. Tip the entire contents into a heated serving bowl.

Serves 6–8
Recommended wine:
Greenhough Nelson Sauvignon Blanc

Recipe from Tersha Coppell
THE SMOKEHOUSE, NELSON

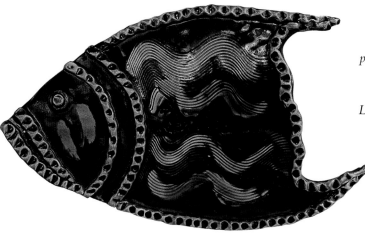

Right: Yachts ride at anchor Mapua, in the Nelson regio Boating is a popular pasti throughout New Zealar particularly in sheltered areas l the Waimea Inl

Left: Fantasy Fish is a sculptu slab work of locally produ stonework clay with copper a cobalt glazes. Ha Bjorklund, originally fr Denmark, has lived in Nels for 30 yea

Mussel and Kumara-stuffed Squid
with seared tuna and curry aïoli

4 medium-sized squid tubes
1 large purple kumara
1kg mussels
2 tablespoons chopped parsley
1 spring onion, chopped
¼ cup freshly grated parmesan
1 tablespoon fish sauce (available at Asian food stores)
zest and juice of 1 small lime
salt and freshly ground black pepper to taste
toothpicks

Clean the squid tubes and remove any purple skin (rubbing with salt makes it easier). Blanch for a few seconds in boiling water, then refresh in cold water. Drain and set aside. Scrub the kumara but don't peel it. Cover with lightly salted water and bring to a gentle simmer. Cook for 8–10 minutes, or until just cooked but still a little firm – it should feel like a ripe pear when a knife is inserted. Remove from the water and allow to cool slightly. Cut into 1cm dice and place in a large bowl.

Scrub and debeard the mussels and steam them in a little water, removing each one as soon as it opens. Remove the mussels from the shell and cut each one into four or five pieces. Add to the reserved kumara and carefully stir in the parsley, spring onion, parmesan, fish sauce and lime zest and juice. Season to taste, being generous with the pepper. After a few minutes, when the flavours have married, secure one end of each squid tube with one or two toothpicks and spoon the stuffing in the other end, leaving plenty of room to secure the other end with toothpicks. Refrigerate until required.

Left: Overlooking Tahunanui Beach, a popular picnic spot. Nelsonians are justifiably proud of their food and wine industries, so the picnic basket is likely to be stocked entirely with local goodies.

Curry Aïoli
1 large egg yolk
1 tablespoon mirin (Japanese cooking sake)
1 tablespoon rice wine vinegar
1 teaspoon green curry paste
1 teaspoon Dijon mustard
¹/₂ teaspoon fish sauce, or to taste
200ml vegetable oil
salt and freshly ground black pepper

Place the egg yolk, mirin, vinegar, curry paste, mustard and fish sauce in a food processor and with the motor running drizzle in the oil, drop by drop at first then in a thin stream. When the mixture becomes smooth and shiny, season to taste and refrigerate.

To complete and serve
1 teaspoon Szechuan peppercorns (available at Asian food stores)
1 tablespoon wasabi powder
1 200g big-eye tuna steak
2 tablespoons olive oil
1 tablespoon light soy sauce

Dry-fry the Szechuan peppercorns in a heavy frypan until fragrant. Grind with a mortar and pestle or spice grinder, or crush with the side of a heavy knife. Mix with the wasabi powder and press into the tuna. Heat half the olive oil until it starts to smoke and sear the tuna for 30 seconds on each side then place on ice to stop cooking. Refrigerate until required.

Brush the squid tubes with the remaining olive oil, season and place in a 200°C oven for eight minutes, turning at least once. Allow to rest for 3 minutes.

To serve, slice each squid tube into four or five slices and arrange on heated serving plates. Brush the tuna with the soy sauce, slice thinly and place alongside. Drizzle the Curry Aïoli over the top.

Serves 4
Recommended wine:
Tasman Bay Pinot Gris

Recipe from Luke Macann

THE BOAT SHED CAFE
NELSON

Stuffed Chicken Leg on a Potato Fritter
with tomato salsa and basil butter

4 large chicken legs
200g skinned and boned chicken thigh meat
salt and pepper
100g clarified butter (see Note)
8 rashers streaky bacon

Separate the drumsticks and thighs and completely bone out the thighs. Chop the other thigh meat finely. Use your finger to widen the cavity left when you removed the major bone from each thigh, season the opening and stuff with the chopped meat. Wrap the skin over the opening and secure in place with toothpicks. Season, brush with clarified butter and roast in a 200°C oven just until the juices run clear, but no longer. Remove the toothpicks and wrap a bacon rasher tightly around each leg.

Note: To clarify butter, heat in a small saucepan and skim off the froth as it rises. Pour the clear butter off the sediment at the bottom and chill.

Tomato Salsa
4 large ripe tomatoes
¹/₂ small red onion
4 tablespoons olive oil
pinch caster sugar
¹/₂ cup chopped Italian flatleaf parsley
1 tablespoon stoned and chopped black olives
1 tablespoon chopped capers
salt and freshly ground black pepper to taste

Cut a shallow cross in the stem end of each tomato and plunge into boiling water for 20 seconds, then into cold water. Peel, deseed, and roughly dice the flesh. Chop the onion. Combine the onion and tomatoes with the other ingredients, cover with plastic food wrap and refrigerate until needed.

Basil Butter
300g butter, softened
2 cups firmly packed basil leaves
1 litre chicken stock, ideally home-made
salt and pepper to taste

Put the butter and basil leaves in a food processor and process until creamy. Boil the chicken stock and reduce to approximately one cup. Remove from the heat and whisk in the basil butter. Keep warm, but no hotter or it will separate.

Potato Fritters
4 medium potatoes
salt and white pepper
100g clarified butter

Peel the potatoes, grate them and squeeze out the excess moisture. Season. Heat the clarified butter in a heavy frypan. Using a 10cm pastry cutter as a mould, form four potato fritters and fry, turning once, until golden-brown on both sides. Drain on greaseproof paper.

To complete and serve
Put the chicken legs in a 200°C oven for a further 10 minutes, or until the bacon is crisp. Reheat the potato fritters in the oven. Place one fritter in the centre of each heated serving plate, cut the chicken leg into three (two thigh pieces plus the drumstick) and arrange on top of the fritter, with the drumstick standing up. Strain the Basil Butter around the edge and top with the Tomato Salsa. Serve with a simple green salad.

Serves 4
Recommended wine:
Waimea Estate Sauvignon Blanc

Recipe from John Appelman

APPELMAN'S RESTAURANT
RICHMOND, NELSON

Below: Nelson artist Grant Scott's Food for Higher Plants *encompasses the protective and nurturing forces of plant life that ensure environmental survival. It is constructed using recycled rust-resistant corten steel with red and matt black paint.*

Roast
Eye Fillet of Beef
with steamed piko piko
and Asian greens

4 tablespoons canola or other low-fat oil
1 stick fresh lemongrass
¹/₂ cup lime juice
200ml beef jus (reduced stock or
unthickened gravy)
4 x 200g pieces beef eye fillet
salt and cracked black pepper to taste

Heat half the oil in a large pot, chop the lemongrass finely and fry over low heat until soft. Add the lime juice and reduce by half, then stir in the beef jus. Bring to the boil, simmer for 5 minutes then pass through a fine sieve. Reserve.

Heat the remaining oil in a heavy frypan and seal the beef on all sides. Place on a roasting dish, season and cook in a 220°C oven for 10 minutes, then allow to rest for 5 minutes.

To complete and serve
4 bunches bok choy
12 piko piko (fern fronds – available from
some specialty food stores)
4 large strips prosciutto

While the beef is resting, trim the bok choy, season to taste and cook in a steamer for 4 minutes. Steam the piko piko at the same time. Place the prosciutto slices in the oven for 3 minutes, or until crisp. Place one pile of bok choy on each heated serving plate, reheat the sauce and drizzle over the top. Slice the beef and arrange over the bok choy. Garnish with the prosciutto and piko piko.

Serves 4
Recommended wine:
Tasman Bay Pinot Noir

Recipe from Nick Haszard
PASSION, NELSON

Below: Dana Rose's
Ancient Rhythms 5 (acrylic on
board) is based on the taniwha
motif. It incorporates the elements
of earth, fire, water and air while
celebrating New Zealand's
cultural diversity.

dana rose

Garden Roast with Gareme

4–6 organic parsnips peeled and cut into bite-sized pieces
1 tablespoon olive or sesame oil
1 sprig thyme, chopped
salt and freshly ground black pepper

Drizzle the parsnips with oil, sprinkle thyme over the top and add salt and pepper to taste. Roast until just cooked. Chef Jan Barnett sometimes serves her organic parsnips with Gareme, a spiced yoghurt and feta dip:

Gareme
3 cups thick, creamy yoghurt
1 large clove garlic
350g soft-style feta cheese
2 tablespoons olive oil
juice of 1 lemon
salt and pepper
$^1/_4$–$^1/_2$ teaspoon cayenne pepper

Line a strainer with a clean tea towel and place over a bowl. Put the yoghurt into the strainer and leave in the refrigerator for 12–24 hours. The whey will drain from the yoghurt, leaving it extra thick and creamy. Scrape it from the tea towel into a food processor, discarding the whey. Peel and chop the garlic and add with the feta. Process until smooth. Add the olive oil, lemon juice, then the salt, pepper and cayenne to taste.

Note: Jan says: 'Make it hot, and make a lot because it's also good with bread.'

Serves 4–6
Recommended wine:
Sunset Valley Vineyard Reserve Pinot Noir (certified organic)

Recipe from Jan Barnett

KIMI ORA SPA RESORT
KAITERITERI, NELSON

Far right: Distinctive agapanthus blossoms bring a splash of colour to the Moutere hills.

A Rugged Region

West Coast

*T*here are a thousand legends about the South Island's isolated West Coast. The locals are known as 'Coasters' and are a fiercely proud lot, as famous for their cynicism about city life as for their indifference to petty regulations they see as irrelevant to their lifestyle.

Their personality reflects the landscape. The West Coast is a rugged place with wind-torn beaches, impenetrable forests and rivers that have been known to swell in minutes, carving new paths as they sweep towards the sea.

Much of the local food is wild. Most famous is whitebait, the collective name given to the infant stage of up to 11 types of fish. Collected in wide nets on fiercely guarded individual spots at the mouths of rivers, these tiny morsels are cooked whole either on their own or, more commonly, bound into an egg-based fritter.

Local lakes swarm with trout, and the forests attract hunters in search of wild boar and deer. Both meats occasionally make it to the tables of local restaurants but mostly they are destined for home consumption. An annual Wild Food Festival offers such unique delicacies as huhu grubs, which look like fat, soft caterpillars but taste vaguely of peanut butter, and barbecued sheep testicles.

There is no West Coast wine industry – many locals prefer to partner their meals with a glass of famous Monteith's beer, while others swear by their particular style of home brew.

But wine does make an appearance in restaurants, where products from around the country are promoted with enthusiasm.

The Coast's isolation has attracted a number of artists and craftspeople, and their work can be seen in galleries around the country. Mini-sculptures and jewellery items are crafted from the famous local greenstone, as well as whalebone, paua and other 'found' materials.

Goldmining was once a major activity on the Coast, and the entire region has the pioneering feel that seems to be a legacy of this activity in many parts of the world. It is a fascinating place to visit.

Inhospitable coastline north of Haast, where beaches are covered with driftwood and greenstone pebbles.

West Coast Whitebait Fritter
on kumara chips with kiwifruit and avocado chutney

Kiwifruit and Avocado Chutney
2 kiwifruit
1 avocado
pinch salt
pinch cracked black pepper
1 tablespoon sugar
1 tablespoon lemon juice

Peel the kiwifruit, or scoop out the flesh. Peel the avocado and remove the stone. Place all ingredients in a blender and process until smooth. Cover with plastic food wrap and refrigerate until needed.

Garlic Aïoli
2 egg yolks
3 cloves garlic, peeled
100ml white wine vinegar
300ml olive oil
pinch salt
pinch cracked black pepper

Place egg yolks in a blender and process until colour lightens. Add garlic, drizzle in vinegar then add the oil, drop by drop at first then in a thin stream. If it separates, start with a fresh egg yolk, drizzle in the separated sauce then continue with the remaining oil. Season to taste.

Kumara Chips
1 kumara
vegetable oil for deep-frying
salt and pepper to taste

Peel kumara and cut crosswise into 2mm-thick slices, using a mandolin or the slicing blade of a food processor. Pat dry with paper towels. Heat the oil until it shows a faint smoky haze, add the kumara slices and deep-fry until golden-brown (the slices can also be shallow-fried in a heavy frypan). Drain on paper towels and keep warm in an oven set to low temperature. Season just before serving.

Whitebait Fritter
3 eggs
150g whitebait
pinch salt
pinch cracked black pepper
1 tablespoon butter
2 tablespoons vegetable oil

Beat the eggs with a fork until well combined. Pick over the whitebait to check for debris, then stir into the eggs. Season. Heat the butter and oil in a heavy frypan, pour the mixture in and stir with a fork until it reaches the consistency of runny scrambled eggs. Allow the fritter to set on the bottom, then transfer to a preheated 200°C oven and cook until golden brown.

To complete and serve
1–2 beetroot, boiled and peeled
2 spring onions, finely sliced
3–4 cherry tomatoes
1 sprig fennel

Cut the beetroot into matchstick-sized batons. Arrange the kumara chips on a heated plate and slide the fritter over them. Spoon a generous dob of chutney on top. Garnish with the spring onions, the beetroot batons, the cherry tomatoes and the fennel sprig. Serve the Garlic Aïoli on the side.

Serves 1

Recommended wine:
Montana Marlborough Sauvignon Blanc 2001

Recipe from Riki Tinirau

GLASSHOUSE RESTAURANT
FRANZ JOSEF GLACIER

Top right: Rough pastures bordered by the Southern Alps.

Above: Whalebone Sculpture *by Turi Gibbs (Ngai Tahu, Ngati Waewae). Turi completed his apprenticeship with Westland Jade at the age of fifteen and is now based at Traditional Jade Company.*

Bagels

1 cup milk
¹/₂ cup warm water
2¹/₂ teaspoons quick-acting yeast
2 tablespoons sugar
3 cups flour
1 tablespoon salt
1 tablespoon vegetable oil
1 egg yolk
1 teaspoon water
1 tablespoon poppy or sesame seeds
2 teaspoons Maldon sea salt

Heat the milk until it is just warm. Combine with half a cup of warm water, then stir in the yeast and one tablespoon of the sugar. Whisk to dissolve the yeast, cover the bowl and leave in a warm place for 10 minutes or until the mixture is frothy. (If it doesn't froth, start again with slightly cooler liquids). Sift the flour and stir half into the yeast mixture, add the salt and remaining sugar, then the remaining flour. Mix to make a firm dough.

Use the oil to lightly grease a large bowl, gather the dough into a ball and transfer to the bowl, turning to coat it all over with the oil. Cover lightly with plastic food wrap and place in a warm spot for about an hour, or until it doubles in bulk. Punch it down to deflate it. (At this point, the dough can be covered and refrigerated overnight if you wish).

Turn the dough onto a floured surface and knead until it is smooth and pliable. Divide it into twelve portions. Take a piece at a time and shape into a smooth round by tightly pulling the top surface to the underside and pinching together, repeating until you have a compact ball. Roll in a circular motion, using the palm of your hand. Flatten lightly to a disc.

Poke your index finger through the centre of the disc to make a hole, then insert your other index finger through the other side. Rotate your fingers around each other, stretching the dough to make a ring with a 4cm hole in the middle. Place on a greased baking tray and repeat with the remaining pieces. Allow to stand in a warm place for about 20 minutes, or until they have risen.

Drop the bagels one by one into boiling water. They must be cooked separately, because if they touch they will stick together. Turn after 15 seconds, boil for another 15 seconds and remove with a slotted spoon. When they are all parboiled, place on greased baking trays. Whisk the egg yolk with the teaspoon of water and use the mixture to brush the bagels. Sprinkle with the seeds and salt and bake in a 180°C oven for about 20 minutes. Place on a wire rack to cool.

Makes 12
Recipe from Margaret Weston
THE SMELTING HOUSE
GREYMOUTH

Note: Margaret uses bagels in many ways at The Smelting House. Her Mediterranean Bagels are spread with salsa verde, hummus, grilled capsicum, feta cheese and olives. Another popular choice pays homage to Thailand with a topping of minced pork cooked with spring onions, garlic, ginger, coriander and chilli sauce.

Left: In Pounamu Tuatara *Turi Gibbs allows the raw materials to dictate the form, which he carves using diamond tools. The work is then polished and the base sandblasted.*

Above: West Coast artist Sue Syme is a graduate of the Otago School of Fine Arts. Sue's recent works in watercolour on paper, including Dinner for 7, *focus on the complexities of human relationships. She also works in oils and print making.*

Fillet of West Coast Turbot with Tapenade

served on kumara choux pastry with spinach and caper cream sauce

Tapenade
200g kalamata olives, stoned
6 cloves garlic, peeled
100g anchovies, preferably packed in oil

Place all the ingredients in a food processor and blend until smooth.

Kumara Choux Pastry
2–3 kumara
¹/₂ cup water
50g butter
¹/₂ cup plain flour
2 eggs
vegetable oil for deep-frying

Peel the kumara, boil in salted water, cool and mash. You should have about one cup. Bring the water and butter to the boil in a saucepan, stir in the flour, remove from the heat and beat with a wooden spoon until the mixture forms a ball. Cool slightly, then beat in the eggs, one at a time, stirring until they are amalgamated and the mixture is smooth. Fold in the mashed kumara. Heat the oil until a faint haze appears, then deep-fry the mixture, one spoonful at a time, until golden. You will need twelve pastries. Drain on paper towels and keep warm.

Spinach and Caper Cream Sauce
250g spinach
1 teaspoon butter
6 shallots
¹/₂ cup dry white wine
juice from a small jar of capers, plus enough water to make 125ml
2 tablespoons capers
500ml cream
juice of ¹/₂ a lemon
salt and pepper to taste

Wash the spinach thoroughly and tear into pieces, discarding the thick ribs. Heat the butter in a saucepan, peel and slice the shallots and fry, stirring, until soft but not coloured. Add the white wine and caper juice and reduce by two-thirds. Add one tablespoon of capers, the spinach and the cream and simmer, uncovered, for 15 minutes. Tip the mixture into a food processor and blend until smooth. Return to the pan, season with lemon juice, salt and pepper and put aside. Reheat just before serving.

To complete and serve
4 boned fillets West Coast turbot
2 parsnips, peeled and sliced lengthwise on a mandolin into wafer-thin ribbons (optional)
vegetable oil for deep-frying

Pat the fillets dry with paper towels. Spread the Tapenade evenly over each and grill for 5–10 minutes, or until just cooked through. While the fish is cooking, deep-fry the reserved capers and the parsnip ribbons until crisp. Drain on paper towels. Place three pastries on each heated plate and arrange the turbot fillets on top. Drizzle the spinach sauce over and around the fish, Garnish with the deep-fried parsnip ribbons, if using, and the remaining capers.

Serves 4
Recommended wine:
Okahu Estate Shipwreck Bay Northland Chardonnay 2000

Recipe from Dudley-Anne Thompson

The Bay House Cafe
Westport

Left: Ian Phillips lives in Hokitika. His Dory in Motion *is constructed from recycled copper with a controlled heat patina with acid and spotting. The eye is a paua shell insert. Ian's work explores other fish species, lizards, weta, dragonflies and seahorses.*

Living Heritage

Kaikoura and Canterbury

*C*hristchurch, the city at the centre of the Canterbury region, is known for its 'Englishness'. Many of the local festivals borrow their themes from Great Britain. Each year, secondary school pupils emulate their counterparts at Oxford and Cambridge Universities with a boat race down the Avon River, and tourists can hire a boater-hat-clad guide to punt them down the same river as it meanders its way through town.

The city even boasts its own 'Wizard' – a local character who has built a career out of dressing in appropriate garb and becoming the centre of attention at countless social and recreational functions.

For years, Christchurch lagged behind other main centres when it came to restaurants and cafés, but that has changed dramatically in recent years. Now, entire streets are devoted to the age-old pastime of enjoying good food and wine while watching the ever-changing 'passing parade'.

Admirers of classical architecture can find much to reward them in this stately city. The solid, Gothic lines of the original Canterbury University, now converted into an arts centre and café complex, and the century-old Renaissance-style Roman Catholic basilica are particular drawcards. Of all New Zealand's cities, Christchurch is the one that can best be described as 'different' – and in the most charming way.

Wine has been made in Canterbury for many years, but recently Waipara, to the north, has been hogging the limelight. The region's crisp, cool nights are ideally suited to aromatic varieties like riesling and gewürztraminer, but the whole gamut of styles is represented, with pinot noir showing particular promise.

Art also plays an important role in Cantabrian social life. The new Christchurch Art Gallery Te Puna o Waiwhetu due to open mid-2003 will house the internationally renowned collection of the Robert McDougall Art Gallery. The Canterbury Museum attracts visitors from all over the country and a stroll through the botanical gardens next door is also a rewarding experience.

It is a pleasant day trip to Akaroa, a coastal settlement that gets its uniqueness from the fact that it was settled by the French. In total contrast is the Kaikoura coast, once nationally famous for the quality of its crayfish, now better known as a whale-watching centre.

Stormy skies over a north Canterbury valley near Hanmer Springs.

Seafood chowder

1¹/₂ kg mussels (about 500g mussel meat)
500g skinned and boned fillets firm fish
5 medium carrots
5 medium onions
2 parsnips
1 celery stick
250g butter
¹/₃ cup dry white wine
1 teaspoon dried dill
1 teaspoon dried thyme
2 teaspoons sugar
¹/₃ cup white wine vinegar
1.5 litres fish stock (available in some
supermarkets, or make your own)
125g flour
¹/₂ cup cream
salt and pepper to taste
10 firm-crusted buns

Scrub and debeard the mussels, and steam them open in a little water. Remove the mussel meat and chop coarsely. Chop the fish into bite-sized pieces. Peel the carrots, onions, and parsnips, destring the celery sticks and cut the vegetables into rough dice. Heat half the butter in a large pot and sweat the vegetables over low temperature for 10 minutes. Add the white wine, dill, thyme, sugar and vinegar and simmer gently for 5 minutes. Add the chopped mussels, fish and fish stock and cook slowly for 1 hour.

In another saucepan melt the remaining butter and stir in the flour. Cook for 5 minutes, stirring continously with a wooden spoon to make a golden roux. Add this to the simmering chowder and whisk for 10 minutes. Add the cream and season to taste.

Slice the tops off the buns and scoop out the centres to make bread 'bowls'. Heat in a 160°C oven until firm and crisp, then pour the chowder into them.

Serves 10

Recommended wine:

Hunter's Sauvignon Blanc

Recipe from Richard and Susan Macfarlane

THE STORE, KEKERENGU

Right: Dining outdoors is a popular pastime for a huge number of New Zealanders and visitors. This scene is at The Store.

Citrus-dusted Bluenose
on balsamic beurre meunière

Citrus Dust
zest of 2 lemons
zest of 3 oranges

Reserve a little zest for garnish, and spread the remainder on an oven tray and place in a 60°C oven to dry for approximately 1 hour. It should be thoroughly dry, but with most of its original colour. Allow to cool then grind in a mortar and pestle, spice mill or coffee grinder until fine.

4 x 250g wedges bluenose or other firm-fleshed fish
salt and pepper to taste
2 tablespoons vegetable oil

Pat the fish dry with paper towels then dip into the citrus dust and sprinkle with salt and pepper. Press the reserved fresh zest into one side of each wedge. Heat the oil in a heavy ovenproof pan and seal the fish on the side with the fresh zest, turn carefully and seal the other side. Place into a 180°C oven for approximately 8–10 minutes or until it is opaque right through. Meanwhile, prepare the Balsamic Beurre Meunière:

Balsamic Beurre Meunière
juice of 1 lemon
few drops Worcestershire sauce
50g butter
few drops balsamic vinegar

Heat the lemon juice over low heat and add the Worcestershire sauce. Shake the pan vigorously while adding the butter bit by bit, but don't let it get too hot or it will split. Continue shaking until the butter is melted and the sauce thickens, then add the balsamic vinegar.

To complete and serve
Drizzle a little Beurre Meunière onto the lightly heated serving plates and place the bluenose fillets on top, with the side into which you pressed the fresh zest uppermost. Garnish with any fresh herb you have on hand and, if you like, an edible flower.

Serves 4
Recommended wine:
Kaikoura Wines Marlborough
Sauvignon Blanc

Recipe from Sheena and Dean Hamilton

FINZ OF SOUTH BAY
CANTERBURY

Left: The Seaward Kaikoura Range looks out over a fishing boat. Watching whales and dolphins from boats is a popular tourist activity in the region, but fishing also plays an important part in the local economy. Despite living in a country where nobody is far from the ocean, New Zealanders eat far more meat than seafood – but the pattern is slowly changing.

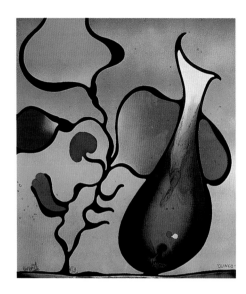

Above: Walter and Brigette Kunz, originally from Switzerland, have lived in Kaikoura for sixteen years and own the Art and Design Gallery. Walter Kunz's, acrylic on board, Olineo (top) uses curved lines as a metaphor for reproduction and the celebration of new life. A Good NZ Red (acrylic on board) revels in the pleasure of socialising and dining with friends while enjoying local wines.

Herb-crusted Canterbury Lamb Rumps
on warm orzo salad

6 lamb rumps (preferably Canterbury)
1 tablespoon vegetable oil
salt and pepper to taste
30g Dijon-style mustard

Trim the lamb rumps of all fat and sinew and pat dry with paper towels. Heat the oil in a heavy frypan and seal the rumps all over. Season, rub mustard on top and put in a warm place to rest.

Herb Crust
150g foccacia or other white bread
20g fresh herbs (rosemary, mint, parsley, etc)
zest of 1 small lemon
zest of 1 small orange
1 teaspoon capers
2 teaspoons olive oil
salt and pepper

Slice the bread and grill, bake or toast until dry. Process to fine crumbs in a food processor. Roughly chop the herbs and add them with the other ingredients to a food processor. Pulse briefly, leaving the mixture slightly chunky. Smear the crust mixture on the lamb rumps and bake in a 180°C oven until medium-rare (approximately 5–7 minutes). Put aside to rest.

Orzo Salad
1 generous cup orzo (rice-shaped pasta)
1 red capsicum (pepper)
1 yellow capsicum (pepper)
1/2 red onion
1 sprig mint
80g peas, thawed and blanched if frozen, parboiled for 3 minutes if fresh
2 tablespoons extra virgin olive oil
salt and pepper

Cook the orzo according to the packet directions (usually around 7 minutes) in plenty of boiling salted water. Drain. Remove the ribs from the capsicums, deseed, slice the flesh and chop finely.

Peel and finely chop the red onion. Roughly chop the mint leaves. Place all ingredients in a bowl and mix.

Mint and Pea Pesto
30g mint leaves
100g parmesan cheese, crumbled
50g ground almonds
100ml avocado oil or extra virgin olive oil
few drops Tabasco sauce
salt to taste

Process all the ingredients in a food processor to form a thick paste, adding more oil if necessary.

Balsamic Syrup
300ml balsamic vinegar
100ml runny clover honey

Stir both ingredients together over low heat until the mixture is reduced by around 50% and has a syrupy consistency.

To complete and serve
24 green olives
160g feta cheese, cubed
50ml extra virgin olive oil

Bake the olives for 15 minutes in a 180°C oven. Warm the Orzo Salad in a frypan, tossing well. Add the feta cheese just as the salad is removed from the heat and adjust the seasoning if necessary. Distribute the salad among four heated serving plates and place a lamb rump on top of each pile. Slice the remaining two rumps and drape the slices around the edge of each central 'pile'. Dab with the pea and mint pesto and drizzle the extra virgin olive oil and balsamic syrup around the edges. Distribute the roasted olives evenly among the servings.

Serves 4
Recommended wine:
Daniel Schuster Twin Vineyards Pinot Noir

Recipe from Andrew Brown

Nor'wester Cafe and Bar
Amberley
North Canterbury

Baked Vanilla and Apricot Semolina

500ml full cream milk
¹/₂ vanilla pod
2 tablespoons sugar
150g dried apricots
60g semolina

Combine the milk, vanilla pod and sugar and bring to the boil. Roughly chop the apricots while the mixture is heating. Turn the mixture to a simmer and slowly trickle in the semolina, stirring constantly until it reaches the consistency of porridge. Remove from the heat, cool slightly then fold in the apricots. Pour the mixture into a shallow tray, spread to a thickness of about 2.5cm and put aside. When it is completely cool use a cookie cutter to shape twelve 5cm rounds.

Toasted Muesli Wafers
3–4 egg whites, depending on size
100g icing sugar
100g flour
80g butter
¹/₄ cup toasted muesli (any good commercial brand)

Beat the egg whites until they form soft peaks. Add the icing sugar and beat until smooth, then the add flour, once again beating until smooth. Melt the butter and add the dry ingredients, beating until everything is well combined. Spoon into a container, cover and refrigerate until 30 minutes before you intend to complete the preparations. Meanwhile, roughly chop the toasted muesli. Remove the egg white mixture from the refrigerator and spread very thinly (2mm at most) on a baking tray. Sprinkle the muesli over the top. Bake in a 180°C oven until the mixture sets (approximately 5 minutes), then remove and cut into twelve long triangles. Return to the oven and continue to bake until golden brown. Remove and cool.

Charred Apricots
12 ripe fresh apricots
200ml sweet white wine

Split the apricots in half, following the natural seam, and remove the stone. Heat a ridged grill pan and use it to make striped char marks on both sides of twelve halves. Place the remaining halves in a food processor with the wine and process until smooth, adding a little water if necessary. Force through a fine strainer into a bowl and reserve.

To complete and serve
60g butter
tips from 4 mint sprigs
1 tablespoon icing sugar

Heat a large, heavy frypan to medium and add the butter. When it has finished bubbling pan-fry the twelve semolina discs, turning once, until they are golden brown. Stack the discs three-high on four serving plates. Spoon the puréed apricot around the edge and arrange the char-grilled halves in a neat pile in front. Garnish with the muesli wafers and mint tips and finish with a sprinkling of icing sugar.

Serves 4

Recommended wine:

Pegasus Bay Aria Late Picked Riesling

Recipe from Hamish Brown

THE GEORGE HOTEL
CHRISTCHURCH

Above: Wendy Wadworth has worked as an artist for 20 years. Rest (top), oil on board, captures the immense, expansive vista of the Canterbury Plains, the largest area of fertile, flat land in New Zealand. Her recent travel overseas motivated her to rediscover her own country, and she returned wanting to paint as she felt. Old Boundary, oil on board, is a response to this new understanding.

Below: The picturesque Christchurch Botanic Gardens provide a serene setting for strolling Cantabrians.

Pressed Coriander Oxtail
with ginger-pickled sweet cucumber

1 medium onion
1 carrot
1 stick celery
$^1/_2$ leek
100g fresh ginger
4 cloves garlic
1 bunch coriander
1–2 small red chillies
1kg oxtail (large pieces)
4 cups plain flour
1 tablespoon chilli oil
zest and juice of 1 lime
$1^1/_2$ litres dry white wine
250ml Japanese soy sauce
500ml mirin (Japanese cooking sake)
1 cup soba noodles (enough to make 2 cups when cooked)
$^1/_4$ cup dry breadcrumbs
2 eggs
1 cup plain flour
3 tablespoons soy oil

Peel and dice the onion, carrot, celery and white part of the leek. Peel the ginger and garlic and chop very finely. Chop the coriander. Remove the seeds and ribs from the chillies and chop finely.

Dust the oxtail with three cups of the flour and brown in the chilli oil. Remove from the pan, drizzle in a little more chilli oil if necessary and add the onion, carrot, celery and leek. When browned add the ginger, garlic, coriander and chillies. Stir for a minute or so, then add the lime juice and zest, wine, soy sauce and mirin. Bring to a simmer then return the oxtail to the pan. Cover loosely and braise in a 180°C oven for $3^1/_2$ hours, or until the meat is beginning to fall off the bone. Remove the oxtail from the cooking juices and allow to cool slightly. Strip the meat from the bones and mix with a little of the strained cooking liquid. Place in a shallow container large enough to enable a plate or board to be placed on top. Weigh down with a can or two and press in the refrigerator for 24 hours.

Meanwhile, cook the soba noodles in boiling water according to the directions on the packet, drain and refrigerate. The noodles will dry as they chill, and can then be cut into small pieces. Mix with the breadcrumbs.

When the oxtail is cool, slice into whatever shapes you like (it will have set into a sort of brawn). Beat the eggs. Dip the slices in the remaining flour, then the eggs, and finally into the noodle/breadcrumb mix. Heat the soy oil and pan-fry until golden brown.

Ginger-pickled Cucumber

¹/₂ telegraph cucumber, peeled
¹/₂ cup cane sugar
100g fresh ginger, chopped very finely
1 small red chilli, deseeded and chopped
200ml Prenzel sauvignon blanc vinegar (or white wine vinegar)
2 teaspoons Prenzel basil oil

Slice the cucumber paper-thin and drain on paper towels. Crush the cane sugar. Simmer everything except the cucumber for 10 minutes, place the cucumber in a bowl and pour the hot liquid over the top. Refrigerate overnight.

Spiced Nut Salad

¹/₂ cup each cashew nuts and peanuts roasted
100g crystallised ginger, chopped
2 tablespoons coriander leaves, chopped
¹/₂ red onion, peeled and chopped
2 teaspoons Prenzel basil oil
4 teaspoons soy bean oil
2 teaspoons rice vinegar

Mix all ingredients together, tossing well. Arrange a few slices of oxtail on a plate and serve with Ginger Pickled Cucumber and Spiced Nut Salad.

Serves 4–6
Recommended wine:
Black Estate Waipara Pinot Noir

Recipe from Phillip Kraal
LE BON BOLLI, CHRISTCHURCH

Top: The fountain outside The Arts Centre of Christchurch is a popular meeting place for locals and visitors alike.

Roast Beef Fillet
with pan-fried potatoes, prosciutto, beans and Spanish onion

54 small green beans
6 medium-sized waxy potatoes
18 wafer-thin slices prosciutto
small bunch basil
100ml safflower oil
1 large red onion
2 large mild chillies
2 cloves garlic
1 tablespoon treacle
2 tablespoons cider vinegar
salt and pepper to taste
1 small bunch chives

Trim the beans and cook in well-salted boiling water until done to your liking (from 1–9 minutes). Refresh in cold water. Peel the potatoes, place in a pot of well-salted cold water and bring to the boil. Cook to the halfway stage (about 10 minutes), refresh in cold water and slice into 3mm discs. While the potatoes are cooking, make eighteen parcels by wrapping the prosciutto slices around three beans apiece.

Blanch the basil leaves in salted boiling water for 30 seconds, refresh in cold water and pat dry. Place in a blender with the safflower oil and process until very fine and green (the basil oil can be used immediately, or left to settle overnight so that the clear oil can be tipped off the solids).

Slice the onion very finely, deseed and slice the chillies and cook both in basil oil until the onion is soft. Peel and chop the garlic and add to the pan, cook for 1 minute then stir in the treacle and vinegar. Season lightly and reduce until almost no liquid remains. Cool to room temperature, chop the chives and stir them into the onion relish.

To complete and serve
6 x 180g beef eye fillet steaks
Maldon sea salt and cracked black pepper
basil oil
2 cloves garlic
200ml jus (reduced stock or gravy)

Trim the meat of all fat and sinew. Season. Heat a little oil until very hot and sear the steaks. Rub each with a cut garlic clove then transfer to a 200°C oven and cook to your preferred degree of doneness.

Meanwhile, pan-fry the potato slices and beans in a little oil until the potato is golden and the ham wrappings around the beans are crisp. Heat the jus.

Arrange a few slices of potato on heated plates, with three bean parcels on top of each. Place the steaks on top of the beans and spoon a little of the red onion relish on top of each. Drizzle jus around the edge and serve.

Serves 6
Recommended wine:
Waipara Springs Cabernet Sauvignon

Recipe from Darryl Maffey
BARCELONA, CHRISTCHURCH

Below: Commissioned by the Christchurch City Council, The Reintroduction of the Fabulous Races *is a collaborative work by Christchurch artist Bing Dawe and blacksmith Noel Gregg. It is situated in Market Square at the Arts Centre. 'Bing's concept for the children's play sculpture was seven connected barriers, each representing a figure from the "fabulous races" of Greek mythology.'*

Beef Fillet Wrapped in Bacon
topped with Kikorangi blue cheese

4 x 180g beef eye fillet steaks
4 rashers streaky bacon
300g green beans
1 teaspoon salt
1 large kumara
2 cups vegetable oil
1/3 cup olive oil
1 medium onion
2 cloves garlic
500ml chicken stock
4 bay leaves
30g brown sugar
20g turmeric
250g couscous
salt and pepper to taste

Trim the steaks of all fat and sinew. Remove and discard the rind from the bacon and use one rasher to wrap around the circumference of each steak, securing with string or toothpicks. Remove the stems from the beans but leave the little tail attached. Bring a large pot of water to the boil, add salt and boil the beans to your preferred degree of doneness. Drain and put aside. Peel the kumara and use a mandoline or cheese slicer to shave lengthwise into thin strips. Heat the vegetable oil and deep-fry the strips until they are crisp and golden (be careful – they burn easily). Place on paper towels and salt lightly.

Heat one tablespoon of the olive oil in a heavy frypan and cook the steaks for 8–12 minutes, or to your liking (rare or medium-rare is best for beef), turning once. Put aside in a warm place to rest, but don't clean the pan.

Peel and finely chop the onion and garlic. Bring the chicken stock to the boil with the bay leaves, sugar and turmeric. Reduce to a slow simmer and drizzle in the couscous. Cook for no more than two minutes, or until the liquid is absorbed. Stir in three tablespoons of olive oil, plus a little more chicken stock if necessary to moisten, and season to taste.

Reheat the beans by tossing in the remaining olive oil.

To complete and serve
$^1/_2$–1 cup beef stock or glaze
40 pink peppercorns
4 thin slices Kikorangi blue cheese
4 sprigs green-leafed thyme, for garnish

Add the beef stock or glaze to the pan in which you cooked the steaks and stir in all the brown bits over a high heat. Add the pink peppercorns and reduce to a good pouring consistency. Place a pile of couscous on each heated serving plate. Put a sliver of blue cheese on top of each steak, and place on top of the couscous. Pour the peppercorn glaze around the edge, garnish with a thyme sprig and serve with the green beans.

Serves 4
Recommended wine:
Pegasus Bay Cabernet
Sauvignon/Merlot

Recipe from Martin Weiss

ROTHERHAMS OF RICCARTON
CHRISTCHURCH

Top left: A braided North Canterbury river on the plains near Hanmer Springs.

Left: Chalice, by Christchurch sculptor Neil Dawson, is an 18-metre conical aluminium sculpture in Christchurch's Cathedral Square. The title and location of Chalice acknowledge a spiritual theme and strengthen the notion of community spirit. The installation celebrated Canterbury's 150th anniversary and the dawning of the new millennium. The 42 aluminium leaves from native trees reinforced with triangular steel 'branches' form a hexagonal design. The work is finished in car paint: silver on the exterior and metallic blue on the interior.

Bruschetta 'Pan Italia'

1 small ciabatta loaf
1 perfectly ripe, full-flavoured tomato,
preferably grown outdoors
1 clove garlic
1 sprig fresh basil
1 ball bocconcini
1 tablespoon extra virgin olive oil
(Pan Italia uses Athena's)
Maldon sea salt
freshly ground black pepper

Cut the ciabatta loaf in half lengthwise and place, cut-side uppermost, under a grill for about 3 minutes or just to heat through and brown slightly. Meanwhile, cut the tomato and bocconcini into 2mm-thick slices, peel the garlic and tear the leaves from the basil sprig, discarding the stem. When the ciabatta has cooled slightly rub both cut surfaces with the garlic, using about half the clove. Spread the tomato over the top followed by the bocconcini and basil. Repeat the layers, making sure you end up with the bocconcini on top. Place the bread back under the grill, not too close, and cook for 4–7 minutes, or until it is golden brown. Place a couple of fresh basil leaves on top of each half, drizzle with extra virgin olive oil and season to taste.

Serves 1 (generously!)
Recommended wine:
Muddy Water Waipara
Pinot Noir

Recipe from Phillip Nordt
PAN ITALIA, CHRISTCHURCH

Note: Phillip says he enjoys this delicious 'snack' alone, when he comes home ravenously hungry after a big day of wheeling and dealing. 'I take the first bite, then I pour a bicciero (mug) of red wine and sip,' he says. 'That's my tea — until the family comes home, of course!' To check that the tomato is really ripe, he smells it to see if it has a 'tobacco' aroma.

Watercolourist Adrienne Pavelka is committed to the theme of the local landscape. The subtle hues of Evening Light
(above) capture the delicacy of changing light and atmospheric conditions. Adrienne is a working member of the
Centre of Contemporary Art and has been a landscape artist since 1979. She has exhibited in Canada and
throughout New Zealand and has works in the collection of the Ashburton Art Gallery. Her Lindis watercolour
(below) captures the terrain of the scenic Lindis Pass on the inland route from Christchurch to Queenstown.

Ginger-scented Scallops
with avocado salad and vegetable wafers

Vegetable Wafers
2 carrots
2 small beetroot
2 small or 1 large kumara
2 parsnips
2 tablespoons vegetable oil

Peel the vegetables and slice as thinly as possible. Heat one tablespoon of the olive oil and shallow-fry in batches until just cooked. Cool slightly, heat the remaining oil and shallow-fry again until bone-dry and crisp. Salt lightly and keep warm.

Avocado Salad
2 avocados
1 small onion
2 medium tomatoes
2 teaspoons sweet chilli sauce (any good commercial brand)
4 sprigs coriander
juice of 1/2 lemon
salt to taste

Cut the avocado in half and remove the stone and peel. Dice the flesh. Peel and cut the onion and chop finely. Remove and discard the stem of the tomato and chop the flesh finely. Mix all ingredients together, salt to taste, cover and put aside.

To complete and serve
32 scallops
1cm piece fresh ginger
2 tablespoons Kikkoman soy sauce
2 tablespoons vegetable oil
1 tablespoon avocado oil

Remove and discard the hard 'boot' from the side of each scallop opposite the roe. Peel the ginger and chop finely, then combine with the soy sauce. Dip the scallops in the mixture and drain. Heat the vegetable oil in a heavy frypan and sear the scallops a few at a time. The exact cooking time will depend on size, but they should need no more than

30 seconds per side. Drain any excess liquid from the avocado salad and pile onto four serving plates. Arrange the vegetable wafers over the top and the seared scallops around the outside. Drizzle the avocado oil around the edge of the plate in whatever pattern you choose.

Serves 4
Recommended wine:
Morworth Estate Marlborough Chardonnay
Recipe from Charles Morkane

Morworth Estate Vineyard
Christchurch

Left: Brigette Kunz is a gilder by trade and uses genuine gold leaf (18–22 carat). Pacific Rose is constructed from recycled customwood covered with layers of gesso, with a paua shell and greenstone insert and finished in 18-carat green gold gilt.

Above: The spectacular Lindis Pass marks the southern edge of the Mackenzie country, which is named after a notorious 19th century Scottish sheep rustler.

A Taste for Adventure

Queenstown and Central Otago

*T*hose who get their kicks from jumping off a bridge with a giant elastic band tied around their ankles or skimming past rocky canyon walls in a speeding jetboat can satisfy their urges in the region surrounding Queenstown.

Originally, it was skiing that attracted tourists in their thousands to this picturesque part of the country, but now this is considered a sedate pastime compared to some of the dozens of other activities dreamed up by thrill-loving entrepreneurs.

Like Rotorua in the North Island, Queenstown is a mecca for tourists, and locals have responded to their needs with restaurants and cafés to suit all tastes.

The local wine industry is at an exciting stage. Central Otago is the fastest-growing wine region in the country and it is rapidly gaining an international reputation, particularly for pinot noir and riesling. Local vineyard owners are a hardy lot. Their vineyards are the southernmost in the world, which means frost is a major worry, but the cold weather is balanced by some of the country's hottest days. The grapes seem to thrive in this climate of extremes. Central Otago wines are among New Zealand's most impressive, and many have won top awards here and overseas.

Gold once played an important part in the local economy, and panning in the shallows of the region's many rivers is still a popular pastime. Locals are proud of their history, and regularly recreate the boom times with village festivals and theatrical events.

There is much for history lovers to admire. Stone cottages are everywhere, many dating back a century or more. The cottages have proved popular with city refugees, but several are also used as weekend retreats by artists and craftspeople who take their inspiration from the rugged landscape.

Queenstown buzzes in the skiing season, but it would be a pity if visitors stayed around the city. The local countryside has a great deal to offer wine and food enthusiasts as well as those with a fascination for the past.

Overlooking Queenstown and Lake Wakatipu, one of the country's most popular all-round resorts.

Pan-seared Salmon on Baked Polenta
with wilted spinach, fennel salad and saffron emulsion

Baked Polenta
3 cups chicken stock, preferably home-made
1 cup polenta
100g butter
100g freshly grated parmesan
salt and freshly ground black pepper to taste
2 teaspoons olive oil

Dilute the chicken stock with three cups of water and bring to the boil. Drizzle in the polenta, whisking continuously. Return to a slow simmer and cook over very low heat for about 25 minutes, stirring often, until it is thick and smooth (be careful – it spits). Fold in the butter and parmesan and season to taste. Brush a baking tray with the olive oil and spread the polenta evenly over the surface. Refrigerate.

Fennel Salad
1 fennel bulb
3 spring onions
1–2 carrots, depending on size

Trim the fennel bulb and spring onion, discarding most of the green leaves. Peel the carrot. Cut all three vegetables into matchstick-sized pieces, place in a bowl and cover with cold water. Refrigerate.

Saffron Emulsion
50g butter
1–2 shallots or ¹/₄ red onion
(approximately 30g)
100ml dry white wine
2 tablespoons lemon juice
pinch saffron
2 tablespoons cream
salt and pepper

Cut the butter into 1cm cubes and refrigerate. Chop the shallots or onion finely, place in a pot with the wine, lemon juice and saffron, and simmer over low heat until syrupy. Add the cream and simmer, stirring, for 1–2 minutes. Remove from the heat and

whisk in the diced butter, bit by bit. Season, force through a strainer and keep warm, but not hot.

To complete and serve
300g spinach
3–4 tablespoons olive oil
4 salmon steaks, approximately 150g each
pinch sea salt
grated zest of 1 orange
4 sprigs chervil or similar herb for garnish

Wash and dry the spinach and remove and discard the stems. Tear the leaves into rough pieces. Cut the polenta into four rounds 14–16cm in diameter. Heat two tablespoons of the olive oil in a heavy frypan and cook the polenta discs, turning once, until they are golden brown on both sides. Keep warm on heated serving plates. Add more oil to the pan if necessary and sear the salmon steaks over medium heat until they are just cooked. They should be medium-rare. Remove and keep warm.

Add more oil to the pan if necessary and cook the spinach with a little salt and the orange zest. Toss quickly and, as soon as the leaves are slightly wilted but still bright green, spoon onto the polenta discs. Top each pile of spinach with a salmon steak. Drain the Fennel Salad, toss in a little oil and sprinkle over the top. Drizzle the Saffron Emulsion around the edge and garnish with the chervil sprigs.

Serves 4
Recommended wine:
Peregrine Pinot Noir

Recipe from Stuart Penn

BLANKET BAY LODGE
QUEENSTOWN

Left: This spectacular setting is home to luxurious Blanket Bay Lodge.

Seared Tuna
with charred vegetables, avocado salad and smoked tomato aïoli

Smoked Tomato Aïoli
1 clove garlic
100g smoked tomato flesh (see page 189)
250ml mayonnaise, preferably home-made
Maldon sea salt and white pepper to taste

Peel and chop the garlic clove and place in a blender or food processor with the tomato and mayonnaise. Purée and season to taste. Reserve.

To make your own mayonnaise, place two egg yolks in a blender or food processor and whisk until they lighten in colour. Drizzle in a cup of olive or vegetable oil, or a mixture of the two, drop by drop at first then in a thin stream. If the mixture separates, start with a fresh egg yolk, drizzle the turned sauce into it, then continue with the remaining oil. Season to taste.

Charred Vegetables
Use whatever vegetables are in season – for example:
2 parsnips
2 carrots
1 eggplant (aubergine)
2 courgettes (zucchini)
2 spring onions or baby leeks
2 tablespoons olive oil
Maldon sea salt and cracked black pepper

Peel the carrots and parsnips, cut in two lengthwise and parboil for 5 minutes, or until they are part-cooked but still firm. Slice the eggplant into 1cm-thick strips, lengthwise or crosswise. Cut the courgettes into halves lengthwise. Salt the eggplant and courgettes and place, salted-side down, on paper towels for 15 minutes. Cut the spring onions or leeks in half lengthwise, discarding most of the green tops. Brush all the vegetables with olive oil and cook on a ridged frypan until just cooked. Keep warm.

Avocado Salad
1 teaspoon cumin seeds
3 sprigs coriander
1/2 red onion
2 avocados
2 teaspoons lemon juice
2 teaspoons sweet chilli sauce (any good commercial brand)

Dry-fry the cumin seeds until fragrant. Coarsely chop the coriander leaves and finely slice the red onion. Cut the avocado in two, remove the stone and skin and dice the flesh. Mix with the lemon juice, then toss with the other ingredients. Cover with plastic food wrap and reserve.

To complete and serve
4 tuna steaks, 200g each
Maldon sea salt and cracked black pepper
2 tablespoons olive oil
3 tablespoons basil oil
3 tablespoons balsamic vinegar

Pat the tuna steaks dry and season. Heat the olive oil until it smokes, then sear the tuna steaks on all sides. Place in a warm oven to heat through without further cooking (they should remain rare). Place a small PVC cylinder or other open-ended mould in the centre of each serving plate. Spoon Avocado Salad into the moulds, then carefully lift them off. Arrange the vegetables on top, then the tuna steaks. Spoon a little Smoked Tomato Aïoli over each steak and drizzle with the basil oil and balsamic vinegar.

Serves 4
Recommended wine:
Felton Road Chardonnay

Recipe from Michael Chambers

19TH RESTAURANT, STEAMER
WHARF, QUEENSTOWN

Far left: The historic steamer Earnslaw is a Queenstown identity. This beautifully situated resort is home to dozens of restaurants, cafés and brasseries catering for the tourists who flock to the area throughout the year. Local restaurateurs are particularly keen to promote Central Otago wines, many of which are gaining an international reputation. Pinot noir is the grape with which the region has made its name, but many classic varieties seem very happy in the local climate.

Pacific Plate

Vanilla-cured Salmon
100g salmon fillet
rock salt
caster sugar
2 vanilla pods, split

Place the salmon fillet in a shallow container and cover with the rock salt and caster sugar, using about 60% salt to 40% sugar. Refrigerate for 24 hours. Wash the salt/sugar mix off, wipe clean and rub with the split vanilla beans. Refrigerate overnight.

Samoan Oka
100g skinned and boned white fish fillets
juice of 2 lemons or limes
2 tablespoons coconut cream
1 small red chilli, deseeded and chopped
2 sprigs coriander, chopped

Cut fish into 1½cm cubes, toss in the lemon or lime juice and refrigerate. When the fish has been in the refrigerator for an hour, drain off the excess liquid and toss with the coconut cream, chilli and coriander.

Scallops
1 tablespoon avocado oil
3 scallops

Heat the avocado oil until it starts to smoke, and sear the scallops quickly on both sides.

King Prawns
3 king prawns
1 egg
30g dessicated coconut
vegetable oil for deep-frying

Wash and peel the prawns, leaving the head and tail attached. Cut a fine groove down the centre of the back and remove and discard the dark intestinal tract. Whisk the egg and brush it over the prawns. Dip in the dessicated coconut and deep-fry until golden.

Stuffed Squid Tubes
6 mussels, debearded, steamed open and chopped
1 clove garlic, chopped
2 tablespoons fresh breadcrumbs
3 small squid tubes, cleaned
vegetable oil

Mix the mussel flesh, garlic and breadcrumbs together and use it to stuff the squid tubes. Close with a toothpick and brush with the oil. Pan-fry or bake in a 180°C oven until opaque.

Taro Crisps
¼ taro
vegetable oil for deep-frying

Peel the taro and cut into wafer-thin slices. Deep-fry until golden.

Dipping Sauce
1 small red chilli, deseeded and chopped
2 sprigs coriander, chopped
1 teaspoon Thai or Vietnamese fish sauce
1 teaspoon lime (preferably) or lemon juice

Stir all the ingredients together.

To complete and serve
1 teaspoon chopped parsley
1 tablespoon crème fraîche
salt and pepper
1 small bunch watercress

Stir the parsley into the crème fraîche. Slice the reserved salmon fillet as thinly as possible (part-freezing makes it easier). Check all dishes for seasoning then arrange on a platter with the dipping sauce and crème fraîche in bowls. Garnish with watercress.

Serves 1 (generously!)
Recommended wine:
Mt Difficulty Target Gully Riesling

THE COPPER CLUB
QUEENSTOWN

Top Right: Basket of Dreams *adorns Queenstown Hill and delights in views of Lake Wakatipu. It is the destination artwork for 'Time Walk', a project that embodies the message, 'within our history lies our future well-being'. This collaborative public sculpture, commissioned by Queenstown Lake District Council, was designed by sculptor Caroline Robinson and constructed by Springbank General Metalwork. The stone mason was Doug Frew, and Blakely Wallace & Associates were the landscapers. The story panels were created by Design by Dezign.*

Below: Caroline Robinson's Abundance Baskets *are hand-woven from recycled copper wire then burned in an open fire to achieve rich oxidised colourings. Caroline is currently a member of an urban design team working on the Glen Innes town centre redevelopment project for Auckland City Council.*

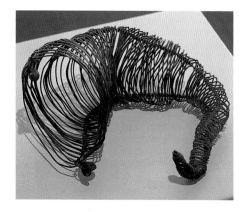

Lemon and Orange Cake
with honey crème brûlée

Lemon and Orange Cake
3 eggs
1 cup sugar
¹/₂ cup water
100g butter
zest and juice of ¹/₂ lemon
zest and juice of ¹/₂ orange
1¹/₄ cups plain flour
pinch salt
1 teaspoon baking powder
¹/₂ teaspoon baking soda

Beat the eggs and sugar together until pale and fluffy. Place the water, butter, lemon and orange zests and juices in a saucepan, bring to a simmer and remove from the heat. Sift together the flour, salt and baking powder then fold in the egg and sugar mixture. Add the baking soda to the water and butter mixture and gently fold this into the cake batter, taking care not to over-mix. Turn the batter into a greased muffin tin and place in a 180°C oven. Bake for 35–40 minutes, or until a skewer inserted into the centre of the cake comes out clean. Cool on a rack.

Honey Crème Brûlée
2 egg yolks
30g sugar
200ml cream
¹/₂ teaspoon finely grated fresh ginger
6 teaspoons liquid honey (ideally from Central Otago)

Whisk the egg yolks and sugar together until the mixture turns pale. Heat the cream and ginger in a small saucepan to a low simmer, remove from the heat and add to the egg mixture in a stream, whisking continuously. Skim off any froth. Place a teaspoon of honey in the bottom of six shot glasses, then slowly pour in the brûlée mixture. Place in a roasting pan and add enough water to reach halfway up the glasses, cover with foil and bake in a 160°C oven for about 15 minutes, or until set but still trembling slightly. Remove and cool.

Candied Orange Zest
zest of 2 oranges
¹/₂ cup sugar
1¹/₂ cups water

Blanch the orange zest in boiling water for 3 minutes, drain and rinse in cold water. Bring the sugar and water to the boil in a small saucepan, add the drained zest, reduce the heat and simmer until the zest turns translucent. Turn the mixture out onto greaseproof paper and allow to cool and set. Pulse the 'toffee' in a food processor until it is the consistency of coffee crystals.

Orange Mascarpone
100g mascarpone
zest and juice of 1 orange
20g icing sugar

Mix all the ingredients together.

To complete and serve
30g soft brown sugar

Sprinkle the brown sugar over the tops of the custards in their shot glasses. Place under a hot grill, still in the water bath, until the tops caramelise. Place each glass on a large serving plate and arrange a wedge of Lemon and Orange Cake alongside. Spoon one tablespoon of Orange Mascarpone over the cake and sprinkle with the candied zest. At Gantley's, the dish is served with honey and cinnamon ice cream and garnished with a vanilla and chocolate tuille twist, fresh strawberries, sauce Anglaise and strawberry coulis.

Serves 6
Recommended wine:
Montana Virtu

Recipe from Jared Aldridge
GANTLEY'S HISTORIC
RESTAURANT, QUEENSTOWN

Left: Queenstown has made a name for itself as the adventure capital of the world. This bridge over the Shotover River is used for bungy jumping while, below, thrill-seekers roar through the canyons in skilfully piloted jet boats.

Left: The Gate *to 'Time Walk' was designed by Anne Wadworth and overseen by Dave Watts of Springbank General Metalwork. The solid mild-steel gate, constructed by Robert Marshall-Smith, welcomes visitors to a 1.7-kilometre track along which elegant story panels reveal Queenstown's history.*

Eye Fillet of Beef
with nori-wrapped hare

800g piece centre-cut Hereford beef eye fillet
1 saddle of hare
3 tablespoons olive oil
1 sheet nori
sea salt and cracked black pepper
crushed juniper berries

Trim the fillet of all fat and sinew. Make an incision from end to end and put aside. Take the backstrap from a large saddle of hare, heat a little olive oil in a heavy frypan and sear it quickly on all sides. It must be very rare, so cook it for no more than 30 seconds. Roll in the nori, then put aside to soften for 4–5 minutes.

Using a gentle twisting motion, screw the backstrap into the incision you have made, taking care not to tear the beef. Reheat the frypan, add a little more oil, season the fillet with salt, pepper and juniper berries and sear it well on all sides. Transfer to a 250°C oven and cook for 20 minutes. Transfer to a warm plate, cover loosely and allow to rest for 5 minutes. Meanwhile, make the sauce.

Cabernet Reduction Sauce
2 shallots
4 cloves garlic
2 tablespoons olive oil
1 cup cabernet sauvignon
1 cup veal or beef stock

Peel the shallots and chop finely. Peel and crush the garlic cloves and chop finely. Heat the olive oil in a heavy pan and cook the shallots until they soften and turn clear. Stir in the garlic but don't let it colour. Add the wine, reduce a little, then stir in the stock. Reduce the liquid by half, or until it is slightly syrupy. Keep warm.

To complete and serve
3 tablespoons unsalted butter
sea salt and cracked black pepper
3 tablespoons balsamic vinegar
2 tablespoons extra virgin olive oil
2 tablespoons chopped fresh herbs (parsley, rosemary, etc)

Whisk the butter, bit by bit, into the Cabernet Reduction Sauce. Work just off the heat and don't allow the sauce to boil. Season to taste. Reduce the balsamic vinegar slightly in a heavy pan and stir in the olive oil and fresh herbs. Cut the fillet into 1cm slices and arrange on heated serving plates. Drizzle with the vinegar and oil mixture and pour Cabernet Reduction Sauce around the edge. Serve with oven-baked potatoes and any green vegetable you fancy.

Serves 4–5
Recommended wine:
Black Ridge Pinot Noir

Recipe from Peter Gawron

SAFFRON, ARROWTOWN
CENTRAL OTAGO

Below: The Crown Range and historic Arrowtown, once the centre of local gold-panning activity.

Venison and Sweet Koura
with chargrilled vegetables

¹/₂ pumpkin
1 orange kumara
1 eggplant (aubergine)
salt
1 green capsicum (pepper)
1 red onion

Peel and deseed the pumpkin and cut into thin slices. Blanch in boiling water until almost cooked, but still firm. Peel the kumara and slice ¹/₂cm thick. Blanch in boiling water. Slice the eggplant into 1cm-thick slices, salt lightly and arrange on paper towels with more on top. Remove the ribs and deseed the capsicum and cut the flesh into flat sections. Peel the onion and cut into quarters, leaving enough of the root end to prevent the layers from coming apart.

Cervena
2 x 250g Cervena Denver leg pieces
2 tablespoons olive oil

Brush the cervena pieces with olive oil and sear in a hot pan for 2 minutes. Place in a 180°C oven for 4–5 minutes, or until cooked medium-rare at most. Allow to rest in a warm place.

To complete and serve
2 koura (freshwater crayfish) or king prawns
olive oil
16–24 green beans
3–4 tablespoons olive oil
sea salt and freshly ground black pepper
4 tablespoons plum sauce
120ml pinot noir or other dry red wine
200ml venison or beef jus (reduced stock)
fresh herbs (chives, basil etc) to garnish

If using koura, boil until just cooked in salted water. Leave whole, but cut away and discard the undershell from the tail to make it easy for diners to get at the meat. If using prawns, remove the shell, but leave the head and tail attached. Cut along the top of the tail and remove and discard the dark intestinal vein. Pan-fry until firm and opaque in a little olive oil. Top the beans, but leave the tail attached, and cook in salted boiling water to your desired degree of doneness.

Brush the other vegetables with olive oil, season with sea salt and freshly cracked black pepper and cook in a frypan or ridged grill pan, or on a barbecue. Add the beans at the last minute just to heat through.

Transfer the cervena pieces to a hot plate and use the pan in which it was cooked to reduce the plum sauce, red wine and jus to a good pouring consistency. Arrange the vegetables on heated serving plates, slice the cervena pieces and sit on top, drizzle the reduction sauce around the edge and garnish with the koura or prawns and the fresh herbs.

Serves 2
Recommended wine:
Chard Farm Pinot Noir

Recipe from Jeanie and Alistair Watson

OLIVER'S
CLYDE

Top left: The road in to Chard Farm Vineyard is perched on the edge of the Kawarau Gorge.

Right: The Blue Lake in historic St Bathans was created by flooding a quarry made by gold sluicing in earlier days.

A World Apart

Otago and Southland

New Zealand is too small to have developed distinctly different regional accents – except in Southland.

Linguists are divided on whether the local tendency to roll the letter 'r' is a result of geographic isolation or a throwback to the region's Scottish ancestry, but there is no doubt that it is becoming more pronounced.

The locals are fiercely proud of their long-time link with Scotland. Distilling so-called Hokonui whisky in the hills behind the township of Gore was once a thriving illicit industry, and oats for use in porridge were once the major local crop.

Generally speaking, New Zealanders don't get enthusiastic about seasonal foodstuffs in the way Europeans do, partly because our relatively mild climate means many delicacies are available all year round. Southland's famous Bluff oysters are an honourable exception. Unfortunately, expediency and freight costs mean these delicacies are removed from their shells and bottled before being shipped around the country. They are still delicious, but a trip to the township of Bluff to sample them straight from the shell should be a must on any oyster-lover's itinerary.

Restaurants in the city of Dunedin and surrounding Southland towns are proud of the wines from nearby Central Otago, and it is often possible to buy small-production lines that are seldom seen away from the winery. As an alternative to wine, Speight's beer is a popular local favourite.

Dunedin boasts one major public gallery and several privately owned establishments featuring the work of local artists. Historical artifacts also play an important part in the permanent exhibitions. Goldmining, sealing and whaling were once vital activities, and much paraphernalia from these enterprises has been preserved for posterity.

Dunedin is the only city in New Zealand that can truly be described as a university town. Otago University attracts students from all over the country and overseas. Nicknamed 'scarfies' because of their penchant for wearing long scarves as a protection against the often bitingly cold local winds, the students are an important part of the local scene.

Hay bales await collection from end-of-summer pastures near Alexandra.

Coconut Bavarois

Bavarois
250ml coconut milk
3 egg yolks
2 drops vanilla essence
60g caster sugar
3 leaves gelatin
250ml cream

Scald the coconut milk in a heavy saucepan. Beat the egg yolks with the vanilla essence and caster sugar until light and creamy. Add a small amount of the scalded coconut milk and mix well. Place over a double boiler (or place the saucepan into a larger one part-filled with hot water), then gradually stir in the remaining coconut milk and cook until the mixture thickens. Soak the gelatin leaves and add, stirring until they are completely dissolved. Pour into a clean bowl, cover with a piece of waxed paper and put aside to cool. Whip the cream until it forms soft peaks. When the egg and coconut milk mixture is just beginning to set, carefully fold in the cream. Tip into eight moulds, cover and refrigerate until set.

Tuile Biscuits
50g plain flour
50g icing sugar
50g egg white
50g softened butter

Mix all ingredients together until completely smooth, with no lumps. Rest for 1 hour. Spread into whatever shapes you like on Teflon sheets (or non-stick baking paper) and bake in a 170°C oven until the edges turn light gold (approximately 3–4 minutes). If you need to adjust the shapes, do so while the tuiles are hot. Allow to cool, then store in an airtight container until needed.

Rhubarb Compote
4 large stalks rhubarb
200ml stock syrup (see Note)

Cut the rhubarb stalks into 4cm lengths. Place in the cold stock syrup, bring to a gentle simmer, remove from the heat and put aside to cool.

Note: To make stock syrup, bring 100g caster sugar, 100ml water and a quarter stick of cinnamon to the boil and simmer for 5 minutes, removing scum from the surface as it rises. Put aside to cool, then transfer to a jar for storage in the refrigerator. Use as required.

To complete and serve
Unmould the Bavarois onto serving plates and spoon Rhubarb Compote over and around them. Place Tuile Biscuits on the side.

Serves 8
Recommended wine:
Ngatarawa Alwyn Noble Harvest

Recipe from Michael Coughlin

BELL PEPPER BLUES
DUNEDIN

Right: Marion Mewburn, originally from Germany, has lived in Otago since 1990. Her ceramic teapot, Angel Pouring Cuppa, is stained and clear glazed.

Above: CC Model *is a steel string guitar by Port Chalmers guitar maker Ian Davie. Ian works with native woods and his complex stringed instruments have an arresting resonance and tonal quality. This guitar has a small body cut away in a classic style. The back and side are heart rimu with a kahikatea and kauri soundboard, a mahogany neck and jarrah fingerboard. His delicate works are finished with Danish oil and Ian's unique formula.*

Saffron-poached Salmon

20 small new potatoes
1 carrot
3 shallots
2 tablespoons olive oil
2 pinches saffron
3 tablespoons white wine vinegar
100ml white wine
1¼ cups fish stock (home-made or commercial sachet)
20 scallops
4 portions salmon fillet
seasonal green vegetables and herbs

Scrub the potatoes, place in salted water, bring to the boil and simmer until just cooked, but still a little firm. Peel the carrot and slice thinly. Peel and roughly chop the shallots. Heat the olive oil in a heavy frypan and sweat the carrot and shallots with the saffron over low heat. Add the vinegar, wine and fish stock and cook until the carrots are soft. Trim off and discard the hard boot from the side of each scallop (usually opposite the roe). Add the scallops, salmon portions and potatoes to the pan and poach until the seafood is just cooked and the potatoes are warmed through. Distribute the potatoes among four heated plates, arrange the salmon on top and the scallops around the edge, along with your chosen vegetables and herbs. At The Hungry Frenchman, the dish is garnished with tapenade-smeared croutons.

Serves 4
Recommended wine:
Chard Farm Riesling

Recipe from René Klein

THE HUNGRY FRENCHMAN
DUNEDIN

Right: Baden French's Beaten Kiwis *are forged sheet steel, hot dipped and lacquered. The works are from a solo show – 'Made in New Zealand' – and are derived from the political climate of 1994–5. Baden is an artist and musician originally from Porirua, now living in Dunedin.*

Terrine of Duck Livers and Wild Pork

500g duck livers
1 tablespoon chopped fresh thyme leaves
¹/₂ tablespoon chopped fresh rosemary leaves
¹/₂ cup Cognac or good brandy
500g wild pork mince (or use farmed pork)
salt and pepper
500g rindless shoulder bacon, thinly sliced

Trim any sinew (the white bits) from the duck livers and discard. Place the livers and herbs in a bowl, pour over the Cognac or brandy and marinate for at least 4 hours. Remove livers, reserving the marinade, and chop three-quarters finely. Put the remaining whole livers aside.

Place the chopped livers back into the bowl of marinade and stir in the pork mince. Season well with salt and pepper.

Line a terrine or loaf tin with the bacon, reserving enough to cover the top. Pour the mixture in a little at a time, distributing the whole livers randomly through the mix. Cover with the reserved bacon strips and a lid, or foil. Place in a baking dish and add boiling water to a level about three-quarters of the way up the side of the tin. Bake at 200°C for 2 hours, topping up the water as required.

Remove from the oven, place on a tray lined with several thicknesses of paper towels and cool. When it gets close to room temperature place a flat weight on top and refrigerate for at least 2 hours.

To complete and serve
Turn the terrine out onto a chopping board. Slice into 1cm-thick slices and serve with crusty bread, a simple green salad and your favourite relish.

Serves 8–10
Recommended wine:
Hay's Lake Pinot Noir

Recipe from Kieran Walsh
FRENCH CAFE, DUNEDIN

Above: This clever mural, Restaurant Scene with Vineyard, *adorns the blank exterior of Dunedin's French Café. The vineyard depicted is Hay's Lake in Central Otago, one of many relative newcomers helping give the fastest-growing winemaking region in New Zealand a big reputation in this country and overseas.*

Salt and Pepper Quail
with cucumber, mango and mint salad, served with palm sugar vinaigrette

Quail Preparation
4 quail

Remove and discard the backbones, cutting along each side with strong kitchen scissors. Lay the birds flat and remove and discard the rib cages and breast bones. Wipe with damp paper towels, pat dry and put aside.

Cucumber, Mango and Mint Salad
½ telegraph cucumber
salt
½ fresh mango
2 tablespoons fresh mint
2 tablespoons fresh coriander
2 tablespoons roasted peanuts

Peel and deseed the cucumber. Sprinkle with salt and rest on paper towels for 15 minutes to drain off excess water. Rinse, pat dry and cut into matchstick-sized strips. Peel the mango and cut into similar strips. Spread both ingredients on paper towels and put aside.

Just before serving, drain any excess water from the cucumber and mango strips. Combine with the mint, coriander and peanuts.

Dressing
½ small red chilli
50g palm sugar (available at Asian food stores)
1 tablespoon fish sauce (available at Asian food stores)
juice of 3 limes

Deseed the chilli and chop very finely. Grate the palm sugar. Mix all the ingredients together.

Palm Sugar Vinaigrette
1 clove garlic
2 coriander roots, or stems and leaves of
2 stalks coriander
1 teaspoon Maldon sea salt
3 tablespoons palm sugar
2 teaspoons sherry vinegar or white
wine vinegar
5 teaspoons red wine vinegar
80ml extra virgin olive oil
freshly ground white pepper

Peel the garlic and place in a mortar and pestle with the coriander and salt. Pound to a fine paste. Caramelise the palm sugar over low heat in a heavy saucepan. Add the sherry vinegar and cook, stirring, for 2 minutes. Remove from heat and allow to cool. Stir the mixture into the coriander paste, add the red wine vinegar and gradually whisk in the olive oil, using a balloon whisk or wooden spoon. Season and push through a fine strainer.

To complete and serve
1 tablespoon flour
Maldon sea salt
freshly ground black pepper
1 tablespoon vegetable oil
salt and pepper to taste
2 teaspoon fried shallots (available at
Asian food stores)

Dust quail all over with flour and season well. Heat the vegetable oil in a heavy frypan and seal the birds until lightly golden. Transfer to a 180°C oven and continue cooking for 5 minutes. Cut each quail in half and place the two halves on top of one another on heated serving plates. Toss the Cucumber, Mango and Mint Salad with the Dressing, season to taste and arrange a pile alongside the quail on each plate, then sprinkle with fried shallots. Place the Palm Sugar Vinaigrette into four small bowls and serve as a dipping sauce.

Serves 4

Recommended wine:

Felton Road Riesling 2000

Recipe from Helen Mason and
Grant Cockcroft

2 CHEFS, DUNEDIN

Above: Richard van Dijk, knifemaker and goldsmith from Hoiho studio on the Otago Peninsula, is a specialist in hard-forged Damascus (laminated steel) knives. The precision, simplicity and elegance of the smooth line give optimum style and functionality.

Artist/jeweller John Robinson's Railway Station *(acrylic and collage on board) explores the railway and Victorian buildings within the historical precinct of Dunedin. This improvisation uses strong, bright colours to reinforce the vitality of Dunedin's community. Robinson's brooches in gold and silver have similar themes.*

Seared Beef and Baby Vegetables
with red onion and sun-dried tomato jam

Red Onion and Sun-dried Tomato Jam
2 red onions
6-10 sun-dried tomatoes
2 tablespoons olive oil
2 tablespoons brown sugar

Peel the onions and chop finely. Thinly slice the sun-dried tomatoes. Heat the oil in a heavy frypan and cook the onions, stirring, until they are soft but not coloured. Add the tomatoes and sugar and cook until lightly caramelised. Set aside to cool.

Seared Beef
4 x 180g beef steaks (eye fillet, Scotch fillet or sirloin)
2 cloves garlic
¹/₂−1 cup olive oil
¹/₄ cup light soy sauce
a selection of baby vegetables (potatoes, carrots, turnips, beetroot, etc)

Trim the steaks of all fat and sinew. Peel and finely chop the garlic. Place in a bowl with the olive oil and soy sauce and add the steaks. Marinate the meat for at least 1 hour or overnight, turning occasionally.
Prepare the baby vegetables and cook in well-salted boiling water to your preferred degree of doneness. Drain. Heat a heavy frypan and sear the steaks all over. Transfer to a 180°C oven and cook to the degree you prefer (beef is best rare or medium-rare). Allow to rest for a few minutes in a warm place.

To complete and serve
2 tablespoons olive oil
¹/₄ cup plum sauce (any good commercial brand)
a few drops avocado oil
4 whole chives, to garnish

Heat the oil in a heavy pan and toss the vegetables to warm through. Arrange on four heated serving plates. Cut the meat

into 1cm slices and arrange over the vegetables, drizzling any juices over the top. Spoon a little Red Onion and Sundried Tomato Jam on top of each slice, and drizzle plum sauce and avocado oil around the edge. Garnish with the chives.

Serves 4
Recommended wine:
Huntaway Reserve Hawke's Bay
Merlot/Cabernet Sauvignon 2000

Recipe from Clayton Hope

BEACHHOUSE CAFE AND BAR
RIVERTON

The stone Nugget Point Lighthouse was built in 1869. Fur seals and Hooker's sea lions are resting on the rocks below.

Grilled Pork Loin
on lemongrass and spinach risotto with spiced plum sauce

Plum Sauce
1 x 450g can Black Doris plums
1 small onion
2 small red chillies
1 tablespoon unsalted butter
salt and pepper to taste

Remove the stones from the plums. Put the juice aside. Place the flesh in a food processor or blender and process until mushy. Peel and finely chop the onion. Remove and discard the seeds from the chillies and chop the chillies finely. Heat the butter in a heavy frypan and add the onion and chillies. Pan-fry until soft but not coloured. Stir in first the juice from the plums, then the pulped flesh. Bring to the boil and stir, then remove from heat. Season to taste.

Lemongrass Sauce
3 tablespoons peanut oil
4 shallots, finely chopped
2 cloves garlic, finely chopped
6 coriander roots, or stems and leaves from 6 stalks, chopped and crushed
2 sticks lemongrass, white part only, chopped and crushed
2 small red chillies, deseeded and chopped
6cm piece fresh ginger, peeled and chopped
1 kaffir lime leaf (available at Asian food stores)
1 cup coconut milk
1 cup chicken stock
3 tablespoons fish sauce (available at Asian food stores)
3 tablespoons palm sugar
juice of 1 lime (approximately 3 teaspoons)
salt and pepper to taste

Heat the peanut oil in a heavy saucepan. Add the shallots, garlic, coriander, lemongrass, chillies, ginger and lime leaf and cook until softened but not coloured. Add the coconut milk and chicken stock and simmer for 10 minutes. Add the remaining ingredients and season to taste.

Pork Loin

6 x 180g portions pork backstrap
enough streaky bacon to wrap the pork
salt and pepper to taste
2 tablespoons olive oil

Remove the pork skin and pat dry with paper towels. Remove and discard the bacon rinds and use the rashers to wrap the pork portions. Season with salt and pepper, remembering that the bacon may be salty. Heat the oil in a heavy frypan and seal the pork pieces all over. Place in a 180°C oven for 5–7 minutes, or until the juices run clear but the meat is still moist. Place aside to rest. Cook the crackling separately until crisp.

Spinach Risotto

700ml (approximately) chicken stock
1 tablespoon unsalted butter
1 small onion, finely chopped
2 cups arborio rice
1 bunch spinach, washed and chopped

Heat the stock to a gentle simmer. Melt the butter in a large, heavy saucepan and cook the onion until soft. Add the rice and stir until it is coated with butter. Add the hot chicken stock a little at a time, allowing the rice to absorb each addition. When half-cooked (about 10 minutes) stir in the Lemongrass Sauce in the same way as the stock. Keep stirring and simmering until the rice is fully cooked, but retains a little bit of bite (20–25 minutes). Just before the rice is cooked, stir in the spinach. Keep warm.

To complete and serve
Spoon a serving of risotto into the centre of each heated serving plate. Pour Plum Sauce around the edge. Cut the pork pieces on an angle and arrange over the risotto. Garnish with the crackling.

Serves 6
Wine recommendation:
Olssen's of Bannockburn Riesling

Recipe from Graham Hawkes

DONOVAN RESTAURANT
INVERCARGILL

Top left: Fishing boats at Riverton, Southland, waiting for the next trip to sea.

Below: The jetty at Riverton is a popular local fishing spot.

Recipes (continued)

Lima Bean Aïoli (FROM PAGE 11)

250g can lima beans
2 cloves garlic, peeled
170ml Greek-style yoghurt (ideally Mahoe)
salt to taste
125g cold mashed potatoes (about 2 small potatoes, peeled and boiled)
65ml extra virgin olive oil

Drain the lima beans and place in a saucepan with fresh water. Cook until tender and place in a food processor with the garlic and yoghurt. Process until smooth, add salt to taste and pulse to mix. Tip into a bowl and add the mashed potato, stir thoroughly to mix, then finally add the olive oil. Force the mixture through a sieve. Thin to a fairly thick pouring consistency with boiling water then put aside to reach room temperature.

Cajun Spice Mix (FROM PAGE 12)

2 teaspoons black peppercorns
2 teaspoons cumin seeds
2 teaspoons mustard seeds
4 teaspoons paprika powder
2 teaspoons chilli powder or cayenne pepper
2 teaspoons dried oregano
4 teaspoons dried thyme
2 teaspoons rock salt
2 tablespoons dried garlic flakes
2 tablespoons dried onion flakes

Dry-fry the peppercorns, cumin seeds and mustard seeds in a heavy frypan until lightly toasted and fragrant. Don't use oil as the dry heat releases the spices' own aromatic oils, but be careful not to let them burn. Place in a food processor and pulse until roughly powdered, or use a mortar and pestle. Mix in the other ingredients, using the food processor if you like, until thoroughly combined and evenly textured.

Celery and Green Pea Sauce (FROM PAGE 12)

2 medium sticks celery
1/2 medium onion
1 tablespoon butter
1/3 cup dry white wine
1 bay leaf
1/2 cup chicken stock (home-made, liquid commercial or a weak mixture made from a cube or powder)
1 scant cup cream
1 cup green peas, fresh or thawed frozen
salt and pepper to taste

Destring the celery and finely slice. Finely chop the onion. Melt the butter in a deep-sided frypan or shallow saucepan and fry the celery and onion until soft, but not coloured. Add the white wine and bay leaf and reduce by half, then pour in the chicken stock and reduce to the same level (if you have used a cube or powder, be very frugal, as the salt content will intensify as it reduces. You can always add more at the end). Add the cream, which will become watery. Reduce until the mixture is creamy enough to coat the back of a spoon, add the peas, simmer for 2–3 minutes and season to taste. Remove the bay leaf.

Preparation Method for Crayfish (FROM PAGE 14)

To prepare crayfish, place one hand around the shell just behind the claws, holding with the thumb and middle finger. Use the rest of your arm to apply weight to the crayfish's body as you push a heavy knife between the eyes, cutting right through to the other side (it will die instantly). Work the knife down to finish the front half of the cut. Turn the crayfish around and continue cutting through the tail. Remove and discard the brain and intestines.

Béarnaise Sauce (FROM PAGE 14)

1 shallot, finely chopped
2 tablespoons tarragon vinegar (preferably) or white wine vinegar
2 tablespoons dry white wine
2 teaspoons fresh tarragon if available, or 1 teaspoon dried tarragon
3 egg yolks
200g butter, at room temperature
salt and pepper

Place the shallot, vinegar, wine and herbs in a small pot and cook until the mixture is reduced to a thick paste. Allow to cool slightly then transfer to the top half of a double boiler. Add the egg yolks and one tablespoon cold water and stir vigorously, using a balloon whisk or wooden spoon, until the eggs lighten in colour and go fluffy. Add the butter bit by bit, stirring briskly after each addition. Don't let the mixture get too hot, or you will end up with buttery scrambled eggs. Force the sauce through a strainer, season to taste and put aside in a warm place.

Lemon-infused Avocado Oil (FROM PAGE 17)

To make lemon-infused avocado oil, add the grated rind of one lemon to a bottle of avocado oil.

Sweet Paprika Couscous (FROM PAGE 42)

1 shallot
2 tablespoons olive oil
1 cup Israeli couscous (large-grained – not the instant type)
1/2 cup dry white wine
1/2 teaspoon sweet paprika
pinch salt
2–3 cups (approximately 700ml) fish stock (available at some supermarkets)

Finely chop the shallot and fry in one tablespoon of oil until soft but not coloured. Add the couscous, stir for a minute, then add the wine and paprika. Simmer to reduce slightly, season to taste, then add the fish stock. Simmer until almost cooked (8–12 minutes). Remove and keep warm.

Coriander Sauce (FROM PAGE 58)

1 cup each fresh coriander, mint and basil leaves
2 bunches spring onions, trimmed of roots and some green tops
2 teaspoons grated lime zest
1 cup salad oil

Purée all the ingredients to a fine paste in a food processor.

Lemon Hollandaise
(FROM PAGE 76)

2 tablespoons lemon juice
2 tablespoons dry white wine
2 tablespoons tarragon vinegar
4 egg yolks
250g clarified butter
salt
Tabasco sauce to taste

Bring the lemon juice, wine and vinegar to the boil in a small saucepan and cook until reduced by half. Transfer to a food processor and add the egg yolks. Process for 1 minute, then slowly drizzle in the melted clarified butter. When a good sauce consistency is reached, add salt and Tabasco sauce to taste.

Vanilla Cream (FROM PAGE 85)

250ml cream
1 teaspoon icing sugar
1/2 teaspoon vanilla essence

Whip the cream, then stir in the icing sugar and vanilla essence.

Lime and Poppy Seed Dressing
(FROM PAGE 91)

1/2 small red onion
1 cup olive oil
1/2 cup lime juice
3 tablespoons poppy seeds
pinch sugar
salt and pepper to taste

Finely chop the onion. Using a balloon whisk, drizzle the olive oil into the lime juice, then add the other ingredients. Finally, stir in the chopped onion.

Mint Salsa (FROM PAGE 97)

1/2 telegraph cucumber
1/2 red onion
1/4 cup chopped fresh mint
2 tablespoons red wine vinegar
1 teaspoon white sugar

Peel, deseed and dice the cucumber. Peel and dice the onion. Mix all ingredients together and refrigerate until required.

Puy Lentil Jus (FROM PAGE 105)

50g puy lentils
4 shallots
1 clove garlic
1 tablespoon olive oil
1 teaspoon tomato purée
1 tablespoon port
salt and freshly ground black pepper

Simmer the lentils for 25 minutes in three cups of unsalted water. Strain and set aside. Peel and finely chop the shallots and garlic and pan-fry in the olive oil until soft but not brown. Add the tomato purée, the reserved stock from the confit and the port. Simmer gently for 5–10 minutes and season to taste.

Colcannon (FROM PAGE 119)

800g Desirée potatoes
100g Savoy cabbage, or curly kale
1 shallot
2 spring onions
50g butter
3 tablespoons milk
1 small bunch Italian flatleaf parsley
salt and pepper

Peel the potatoes and place in a saucepan of salted water. Bring to a slow simmer and cook until soft. Chop the cabbage or kale, the shallot and the spring onions. Blanch in salted boiling water and drain well. When the potatoes are soft, strain, place back in the pan and shake over low heat to dry. Warm the butter and milk together and mash with the potatoes. Stir in the reserved cabbage mixture, chop the parsley leaves and add, then season to taste.

Smoked Tomato Flesh
(FROM PAGE 165)

At 19th, tomatoes are smoked over manuka chips. At home, use manuka chips or tea leaves in a home smoker or wok. Cut the tomatoes in half horizontally and place on a rack over the smoking material. Cover tightly and smoke for 10–15 minutes, then remove and discard the skin and seeds. You will need four to six medium tomatoes to yield 100g flesh.

Artists, Agents and Outlets

(in alphabetical order, by artist, followed by page number)

RESTAURANT DIRECTORY

NORTHLAND

Kamakura, 60 Tapeka Rd, Russell. Ph (09) 403-7771.

Killer Prawn, 26–28 Bank St, Whangarei.
Ph (09) 430-3333.

Marx Restaurant, Kerikeri Rd, Kerikeri.
Ph (09) 407-6606.

Omata Estate Vineyard Restaurant, Aucks Rd, Russell.
Ph (09) 403-8007.

The Lodge at Kauri Cliffs, Tapene Tablelands Rd, Matauri
Bay, Northland. Ph (09) 405-1900.

Waikokopu Café, Treaty Grounds, Waitangi.
Ph (09 402-6275.

Waipoua Lodge, State Highway 12, 48km north from
Dargaville. Ph (09) 439-0422.

AUCKLAND

Ascension Vineyard, 480 Matakana Rd, Matakana.
Ph (09) 422-9601.

Café Pacifique, Carlton Hotel, Cnr. Mayoral Dr & Vincent
St, Auckland. Ph (09) 366-3000.

Metropole, 223 Parnell Rd, Parnell, Auckland.
Ph (09) 379-9300.

Nick's Wood Fire Grill, 64 Main Rd, Kumeu.
Ph (09) 412-5040.

Number 5 Wine Bistro, 5 City Rd, Auckland.
Ph (09) 309-9273.

O'Connell Street Bistro, 3 O'Connell St, Auckland.
Ph (09) 377-1884.

Partingtons, Sheraton Auckland Hotel & Towers,
83 Symonds St, Auckland. Ph (09) 379-5132.

Soul Bar & Bistro, 204 Customs St East, Auckland
Central. Ph (09) 356-7249.

Te Whau Vineyard Café, 218 Te Whau Dr, Te Whau
Peninsula, Waiheke Island. Ph (09) 372-7191.

The Café, Hyatt Regency, Cnr Waterloo & Princess St,
Auckland. Ph (09) 355 1234

Vista-Vitae, 6 MacIntosh Rd, Little Oneroa, Waiheke
Island. Ph (09) 372-3337.

White Restaurant, Hilton Auckland, Princess Wharf,
147 Quay St, Auckland. Ph (09) 978-2000.

COROMANDEL AND BAY OF PLENTY

Astrolabe, 82 Maunganui Rd, Mt Maunganui.
Ph (07) 574-8155.

Freo's, 1103 Tutanekai St, Rotorua. Ph (07) 346-0976.

Peppertree Restaurant, 31 Kapanga Rd, Coromandel.
Ph (07) 866-8211.

Somerset Cottage, 30 Bethlehem Rd, Tauranga.
Ph (07) 576-6889.

The Fireplace Restaurant & Bar, 9 The Esplanade,
Whitianga. Ph (07) 866-4828.

The Landing Café, Lake Tarawera, RD5 Rotorua.
Ph (07) 362-8502.

Wharf Street Restaurant, 8 Wharf St, Tauranga.
Ph (07) 578-8322.

WAIKATO, CENTRAL PLATEAU AND TARANAKI

Macfarlanes Caffe, 1 Kelly Street, Inglewood.
Ph (06) 756-6665.

Museum Café, 1 Grantham St, Hamilton. Ph (07) 839-7209.

Restaurant Villino, 45 Horomatangi St, Taupo.
Ph (07) 377-4478.

The Bach, 2 Pataka Rd, Lake Terrace, Taupo. Ph (07) 378-7856.

The Gallery, 64c Victoria St, Cambridge. Ph (07) 823-0999.

HAWKE'S BAY AND MANAWATU

Amadeus Riverbank Café, Suite 6, 69 Taupo Quay,
Wanganui. Ph (06) 345-1538.

Anatoles, The Country Hotel, 12 Browning St, Napier.
Ph (06) 835-7800.

Church Road Winery, 150 Church Rd, Taradale.
Ph (06) 844-2053.

Dejeuner Restaurant, 159 Broadway Ave, Palmerston
North. Ph (06) 356-1449.

Legends Café, 25 Somme Pde, Wanganui. Ph (06) 348-7450.

La Postina, The Old Post Office, Havelock Rd, Havelock
North. Ph (06) 877-1714.

Sileni Estates Winery, 2016 Maraekakaho Rd, Hastings.
Ph (06) 879-8768.

Take Five Restaurant & Wine Bar, 189 Marine Pde, Napier. Ph (06) 835-4050.

Vidal Estate Winery, 913 Saint Aubyn St, East Hastings. Ph (06) 876-8105.

WAIRARAPA AND WELLINGTON

Bouquet Garni, 100 Willis St, Wellington. Ph (04) 499-1095.

Café Cecille, Queen Elizabeth Park, Masterton. Ph (06) 370-1166.

Logan Brown Restaurant, 192 Cuba St, Wellington. Ph (04) 801-5114.

Roxburgh Bistro, 18 Majoribanks St, Mt Victoria, Wellington. Ph (04) 385-7577.

Toads Landing, Homebush, Masterton. Ph (06) 377-3793.

Wakelin House Restaurant, 123 Main St, Greytown. Ph (06) 304-8869.

NELSON AND MARLBOROUGH

Appelman's Restaurant, 294 Queen St, Richmond. Ph (03) 544-0610.

Cellier Le Brun, Terrace Rd, Renwick. Ph (03) 572-9953.

Herzog Winery and Luxury Restaurant, 81 Jeffries Rd, Rapaura, RD3 Blenheim. Ph (03) 572-8770.

Kimi Ora Spa Resort, Martin Farm Rd, Kaiteriteri. Ph (03) 527-8027.

La Veranda, Vintage Lane, RD3 Blenheim. Ph (03) 572-9177.

Marlborough Terranean, 31 High St, Picton. Ph (03) 573-7122.

Passion The Restaurant, 322 Wakefield Quay, Nelson. Ph (03) 539-1307.

The Boat Shed Café, 350 Wakefield Quay, Nelson. Ph (03) 546-9783.

The Smokehouse, Shed 3, Mapua Wharf, Nelson. Ph (03) 540-2280.

WEST COAST

Glasshouse Restaurant, Franz Josef Glacier Hotels, State Highway 6, Franz Joseph. Ph (03) 752-0729.

The Bay House Café, 41 Beach Rd, Tauranga Bay, Westport. Ph (03) 789-7133.

The Smelting House, 102 Mackay St, Greymouth. Ph (03) 768-0012.

KAIKOURA AND CANTERBURY

Barcelona Bistro and Bar, Ground Floor, Clarendon Tower, Cnr Oxford Tce & Worcester Blvd, Christchurch. Ph (03) 377-2100.

Finz of South Bay, 103 South Bay Pde, Kaikoura. Ph (03) 319-6688.

Le Bon Bolli, Cnr Montreal St & Worcester Blvd, Christchurch. Ph (03) 374-9444.

Morworth Estate Vineyard, Broadfield RD6, Christchurch. Ph (03) 349-5014.

Nor'wester Café, 95 Main North Rd, Amberley. Ph (03) 314-9411.

Pan Italia, 12 Saxon St, Phillipstown. Ph (03) 381-2435.

Rotherhams of Riccarton, 42 Rotherham St, Riccarton. Ph (03) 341-5142.

The George Hotel, 50 Park Tce, Christchurch. Ph (03) 379-4560.

The Store Restaurant, Kekerengu, Marlborough. Ph (03) 575-8600.

QUEENSTOWN AND CENTRAL OTAGO

Blanket Bay Lodge, Glenorchy Rd, Glenorchy. Ph (03) 442-9442.

Gantley's Historic Restaurant, Arthurs Point Rd, Arthurs Point, Queenstown. Ph (03) 442-8999.

Olivers of Clyde, 34 Sunderland St, Clyde. Ph (03) 449-2860.

Saffron, 18 Buckingham St, Arrowtown. Ph (03) 442-0131.

The Copper Club, Steamer Wharf, Queenstown. Ph (03) 442-7503.

The 19th Restaurant, Steamer Wharf, Queenstown. Ph (03) 442-4006.

OTAGO AND SOUTHLAND

Beach House Café, 126 Rocks Highway, Riverton. Ph (03) 234-8274.

Bell Pepper Blues Restaurant, 474 Princess St, Dunedin. Ph (03) 474-0973.

2 Chefs Restaurant, 428 George St, Dunedin. Ph (03) 477-9117.

Donovan Restaurant, 220 Bainfield Rd, Invercargill. Ph (03) 215-8156.

French Café, 118 Moray Pl, Dunedin. Ph (03) 477-1100.

The Hungry Frenchman, 38 The Octagon, Dunedin. Ph (03) 477-5748.

GLOSSARY

Al dente: traditional Italian term used to describe cooked pasta, literally meaning 'to the teeth'. Now used for both pasta and vegetables cooked to the stage where there is a little resistance or slight crunchiness as you bite.

Arborio rice: a medium-grained Italian rice used in risotto. Use short-grain rice as a substitute.

Backstrap: also referred to as the loin of the red meat.

Balsamic vinegar: specialty of Modena, Italy with a sweet, mellow flavour. Made from specially processed wine then aged in wooden barrels.

Beurre meunière: butter sauce flavoured with lemon and sometimes herbs.

Blind-bake: when making a pastry base without a filling, baking paper is weighted down with rice or dry beans and placed on the pastry to keep it from puffing up while cooking in the early stages.

Bocconcini: small balls of Italian-style mozzarella cheese.

Bok choy: a Chinese green vegetable with white stems and green tops. Readily available in most supermarkets or Asian food stores, or you can use spinach as a substitute.

Bouquet garni: bunch of fresh herbs used for flavouring, tied with string for easy removal.

Broccolini: cross between broccoli and Chinese broccoli or kale with long, thin stalks and small flower heads.

Cervena: a brand name for quality New Zealand venison.

Char-grill: to sear at high heat on a ridged pan, barbecue or special char-grill element. This gives the familiar dark lines or crisscross patterns on meat or vegetables.

Chinese five-spice: ground spice, containing five varieties of spices: fennel, cloves, cinnamon or cassia, Szechuan pepper, and star anise.

Chèvre: goat cheese.

Chorizo: spicy, hot Spanish sausage.

Couscous: fine grains of semolina, used in a similar fashion to rice.

Crème fraîche: cultured sour cream with a high fat content, which does not separate on heating.

Deglaze: after frying, the pan is drained and wine, stock, etc is used to loosen any pan-browned meat and juices to add flavour to a sauce.

Demi-glace: greatly reduced stock, sometimes sweetened with port or sherry. Available at delicatessens.

Destring: to remove 'ribs' from the stalks of vegetables, such as celery or silverbeet.

Dry-fry (or dry-roast): fry in a frypan or roast in the oven without oil.

Dukkah: dry mixture of herbs, nuts and seeds. Most commonly used as a dip for bread dipped in olive oil.

Fennel bulb: round white bulb with green stalks and feathery leaves, similar in shape to celery. It has a crisp texture with an aniseed flavour.

Fish sauce: liquid from salted, fermented anchovies. Thai or Vietnamese varieties are available in most supermarkets.

Gelatine leaves: stiff cellophane-like gelatine best used for fine textured dishes. You can substitute one teaspoon of powdered gelatine for every two leaves.

Harissa: chilli paste made from pounded chillies, garlic, olive oil and spices.

Hokkien noodles: thick, round yellow noodles made from egg. Available fresh in sealed airtight packets or dried in most supermarkets.

Horopito rub: peppery, spicy rub made from the leaves of the Pepperwood tree, ground into a fine powder.

Horseradish: root vegetable with a hot, spicy taste, belonging to the mustard family.

Japanese eel (unagi): long saltwater eel, filleted butterfly-style and basted with Japanese flavours. Available from Asian food stores.

Japanese pickled ginger: thin, pink slices of ginger, most commonly used as a sushi condiment. Available in some supermarkets or Asian food stores.

Japanese light soy sauce: Japanese style, light and naturally fermented soy based liquid.

Jerusalem artichokes: fleshy, irregular-shaped edible tubers.

Jus: reduced pan juices, unthickened or thickened.

Kaffir lime leaves: fragrant leaves from a variety of lime tree. Available dried or fresh in Asian food stores or use lime rind as a substitute.

Kina roe: yellow or orange eggs from sea urchins – small to medium sized kina give the best flavoured roe.

Kirsch: cherry flavoured, brandy based liqueur.

Kosher salt: a mineral salt, like table salt but coarser and additive-free. Will require grinding like sea salt.

Koura: freshwater crayfish or rock lobster.

Maldon sea salt: flakes of sea salt, hand harvested in Maldon, England.

Mandarin-infused oil: olive oil favoured with mandarins. Available in specialty stores.

Mandolin: type of vegetable slicer.

Mascarpone: cream, drained in muslin until solid and smooth – similar in consistency to sour cream.

Mesclun leaves: mixture of salad greens, including rocket (tangy, peppery flavoured green herb), mizuna (dark green, feathery leaf vegetable), oak-leaf lettuce, endive or radicchio. Available pre-packaged or in the fresh vegetable section at supermarkets.

Mirin: sweet rice wine or sake used for cooking.

Nasturium flowers: edible, colourful flowers from annual herb with flat round leaves and a slight peppery taste. Can also be used to add colour to green salads.

Nori: edible, greenish/black dried seaweed sold in paper-thin sheets of varying sizes.

Parisienne baller or scoop: instrument with a sharp round edge used for cutting spheres out of vegetables.

Piko piko: young tip of uncurled native fern fronds. Available in specialty food stores.

Pimiento stuffed olives (also known as pimento): olives stuffed with a small slice of capsicum (pepper), usually red.

Polenta: fine yellow, ground cornmeal used as a porridge-like starch or cooled and fried.

Porcini: variety of highly flavoured, Italian mushroom usually available dried.

Prosciutto: Italian air-dried, raw ham sliced paper-thin.

Puy lentils: dried, dark green lentils from Puy, France. Smaller than whole brown lentils and with a superior flavour.

Refresh: to plunge into very icy water after light cooking to set the colour of vegetables.

Roux: equal measures of flour and melted butter, cooked together and used as a base for sauces.

Roti: unleavened bread made with wholemeal flour and ghee.

Reduction: a liquid which is boiled hard to concentrate the flavours and reduce the volume.

Scald (liquid): to heat to just below boiling to prevent curdling or separation.

Scald (vegetables): to plunge into boiling water to assist with peeling.

Semi-dried tomatoes: tomatoes combined with a special marinade of oils, garlic, herbs and spices and heated to dry. Softer than sun-dried tomatoes but with a more intense flavour than fresh tomatoes.

Shiitake mushrooms: rich brown mushrooms, versatile with a delicate flavour. Available dried, or fresh in some supermarkets. Soak dried mushrooms in warm water for 30–45 minutes, then use as fresh.

Short loin: red meat cut from the top end of the loin, below the ribs (tenderloin or top loin cut).

Suet: solid white animal fat.

Soba noodles: long, round Japanese buckwheat noodles. Brown in colour and available dried in supermarkets and Asian food stores.

Surimi: minced fish off-cuts mixed with a flavour concentrate and artificial colouring, then shaped.

Sushi rice (Koshihikari): Japanese variety of short-grained rice that clings together, perfect for sushi-making. Use short-grain rice as a substitute.

'Sweat': to cook vegetables on a low heat in a little oil or butter without browning.

Szechuan pepper: dried hot and spicy berry used in the province of the same name in China.

Tougarasi (Japanese seven-spice mix): combination of two hot spices and five aromatic spices, dried. Usually includes chilli flakes, citron peel, sesame seeds, nori flakes, and pepper.

Truffle oil: high quality oil infused with truffles, available in delicatessens.

Udon noodles: thick, round white noodles made from flour. Available fresh in sealed airtight packets from most supermarkets.

Vincotto: specialty Italian aged wine vinegar made from the two varieties of grape. Contains no alcohol, acid, added sugar, or preservatives. Use balsamic vinegar as a substitute.

Wasabi (paste or powder): paste of grated flesh from the thick, green root of an aquatic plant, likened to horseradish. Available as a ready-made paste in squeezable tubes or in powder form.

Zest: outer peel of citrus fruit.

WEIGHTS AND MEASURES

For best results when you prepare the recipes, use standard metric measures (250ml cup, 15ml tablespoon and 5ml teaspoon) unless otherwise stated.★ Follow recipe instructions carefully, use level measurements and follow the specified cooking times. The oven temperature table opposite is a guide only. For best accuracy, refer to your own cooker instruction book.

★In NZ, USA and UK,
1 tablespoon = 15ml.
In Australia, 1 tablespoon = 20ml.

Oven Setting Equivalents (to nearest 10°C)

Description	Fahrenheit	Celsius	Gas Regulo No.
Very cool	225–275	110–140	1/4–1
Cool	300–325	150–160	2–3
Moderate	350–375	180–190	4–5
Hot	400–450	200–230	6–8
Very hot	475–500	250–260	9–10

Grams to Ounces: These are converted to the nearest round number.

Grams	Ounces	Grams	Ounces	Grams	Ounces
25	= 1	175	= 6	325	= 11
50	= 2	200	= 7	350	= 12
75	= 3	225	= 8	375	= 13
100	= 3.5	250	= 9	400	= 14
125	= 4	275	= 10	425	= 15
150	= 5	300	= 10.5	450	= 16

1 kilogram = 1000 grams = 2lb 4oz

Liquid Measures

1/4 cup	=	62.5ml
1/3 cup	=	83ml
1/2 cup	=	125ml
1 cup	=	250ml
1/4 teaspoon	=	1.25ml
1/2 teaspoon	=	2.5ml
1 teaspoon	=	5ml
1 tablespoon	=	15ml (NZ, USA, UK)
1 tablespoon	=	20ml (Australia)
1 pint	=	570ml
1 3/4 pints	=	1 litre

To Convert / Multiply By

To Convert	Multiply By
fluid ounces to millilitres	28.4
pints to millitres	568
pints to litres	0.568
quarts to litres	1.136
gallons to litres	4.55
bushels to litres	36.369
ounces to grams	28.35
pounds to kilograms	0.45
stones to kilograms	6.35

General Measures

2 cups flour	=	250g
2 tablespoons flour	=	15g
1 cup sugar	=	250g
1 tablespoon sugar	=	15g
1 cup butter	=	250g
1 tablespoon butter	=	15g
1 wineglass	=	100ml
1 sherry glass	=	70ml

Roasting Meat

(Based on an oven temperature of 180°C/Gas 4–5)

Beef
Rare 20 minutes per 450g, plus 20 minutes
Medium 25 minutes per 450g, plus 25 minutes
Well done 30 minutes per 450g, plus 30 minutes

Lamb
Medium 25 minutes per 450g, plus 25 minutes
Well done 30 minutes per 450g, plus 30 minutes

Pork
Medium 30 minutes per 450g, plus 30 minutes
Well done 35 minutes per 450g, plus 35 minutes

Cake Tins

6in	=	15cm
7in	=	18cm
8in	=	20cm
9in	=	23cm

Loaf Tins

9 x 5in	=	23 x 12cm
10 x 3in	=	25 x 8cm
11 x 7in	=	28 x 18cm

RECIPE INDEX